Mastering Quilt Marking

- *Marking Tools and Techniques*
- *Choosing Stencils*
- *Matching Borders and Corners*

Pepper Cory

C&T PUBLISHING

Copyright © 1999 by Pepper Cory

Developmental Editor: Cyndy Lyle Rymer
Technical Editor: Carolyn Aune
Copy Editor: Vera Tobin
Cover and Book Design: Kristen Yenche
Ilustrator: Jay Richards
Front and back cover and quilt photography by Sharon Risedorph
Back cover quilt by Bonnie Bus

Library of Congress Cataloging-in-Publication Data
Cory, Pepper.
Mastering quilt marking: marking tools and techniques, choosing stencils, matching borders and corners / Pepper Cory.
p. cm.
 Includes biographical references and index.
 ISBN 1-57120-077-0
 1. Quilting--Patterns. 2. Quilts. 3. Stencil work. I. Title.
TT835 .C6797 1999
746.46--dc21
                                              99-6016
                                               CIP
Mylar is a registered trademark of E.I. duPont de Nemours and Company.
Xacto is a trademark of Hunt Manufacturing Company
Contact Paper is a registered trademark of Rubbermaid, Inc.

Published by C&T Publishing, Inc.
P.O. Box 1456   Printed in Hong Kong
Lafayette, California 94549   10 9 8 7 6 5 4 3 2 1

Contents

Dedication

This book is dedicated to two women who have been very influential in my quilting career. One is Marie Moore, my quilting mentor, and the other is Gail Hill, the best hand quilter I know.

Marie taught me precision, patience, and pride in being a quiltmaker. She made her first quilt at the age of seven and hasn't stopped since. When I finish a quilt top, I ask myself, "How would Marie quilt this?" and that thought drives me to design and mark quilting that Marie would praise. Marie, you have my everlasting gratitude.

Gail is a member of a closely knit group of quilting friends called the "Sunbonnet Sues in Canoes", which has met almost every Wednesday night for ten years in Lansing, Michigan. She is a wellspring of good sense, tells terrible jokes, and generally instigates quilting projects in the group. Her courage, good humor, and tiny quilting stitches amaze and inspire us all.

Acknowledgments

Thank you to all of the folks who lent quilts, time, energy, support, good wishes and prayers: All the Sues (you know who you are), Deirdre Amsden, Debra and Aaron Bell, Bonnie Benjamin, Rita Blaugher, Bonnie Bus, Kathy Cannon, members of the Crystal Coast Quilters Guild, Barbara Chainey, Patricia Cox, Beth Donaldson, Alexandra Capadalis Dupré, Philomena Durcan, Linda Fiedler, Mike and Rachel Galyon, Gretchen Blaugher Gockley, Lynn and Will Gorges, Jane Hall, Harriet Hargrave, Beth Holland, Laurel Horton, Roberta Horton, Robert and Ardis James, Nancy Johnson-Srebro, Jeana Kimball, Jane Lury, Sandie Lush, Rod Magyar, Ann Manooch, Judy Martin, Mary Mashuta, Susan McKelvey, Alice Neff, Jeff O'Grady, Dorothy P. Porter, Teddy Pruett, Robert Reeder, Andi Reynolds, Rob Roberts and Betty Boyink Roberts, Elly Sienkewicz, Ron and JoNell Smith, Dorothy Stroud, Cindy Turnbow, Hollis Turnbow, Sue Uncather, and Barbara Woodford.

Detail from Prairie Flower Quilt. Collection of Patricia Cox.

Introduction

This book has been writing itself for years. When I teach quilt marking—my most popular class—I am often asked, "Why isn't there more information on quilt marking?" I can only speculate that we modern quiltmakers are spoiled. There are many books filled with color pictures and illustrated diagrams that show us how to make quilt tops. However, very few books really teach or inspire us to complete the quilt. In my opinion, quilt marking—transferring the designs that will be stitched onto the quilt—is the bridge between making the top and actually getting the quilt done.

Quilt marking is the step in the quiltmaking process that's *not* about color or whiz-bang piecing shortcuts. But for the quiltmaker who relishes the satisfaction of completing her quilts, marking is the perfect time to consider the next phase of the quilt's design—its stitching and the effect of that work on the quilt. The effort of marking goes unseen since only the quilting stitches attract attention. Just as walls cover the beams in a house, quilting stitches will obscure all traces of marking. Marking is the quiltmaker's final manipulation of the quilt top's design. Time spent marking is never time wasted.

Most modern quiltmakers are not aware of the long history of quilt marking, nor that the resultant quilting was a developed needleart as early as the 1400s. While quilted garments and bed coverings exist in many European museums, the needlework traditions of France and England are the two most significant influences on American quiltmaking even today.

The hand-stitched *broderie de Marseilles*, popular from the 1700s into the early nineteenth century, inspired the American white-on-white whole-cloth masterpieces of the mid-1800s. Today we can still buy their descendants as "Marcel spreads"—modern machine-loomed bedspreads—in department stores.

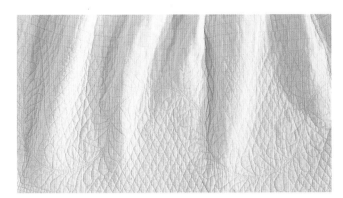

Detail of a Quilted Petticoat. From the author's collection.

The hem of the early nineteenth century hand-sewn petticoat shown is quilted in a running feather design over a background of hanging diamonds. This American garment might have been inspired by a quilted French petticoat called a *jupon*.

Many English emigrants to the United States came from two coal mining regions of England: the North Country (County Durham, Northumberland, and into Scotland) and Wales in the west. These regions had distinctive quilting styles, and naturally the emigrants' quilts contributed to the American style of quiltmaking.

Other quilting influences came from the Amish, a Swiss Anabaptist sect that migrated to the United States in search of religious freedom. The Amish often spent time in the Netherlands and in English ports as they earned passage money to the United States, and traditional older Amish quilts show traces of Dutch and English influence. Looking at pictures of fine antique Amish quilts in books, we consider their beautiful border designs as some of the finest examples of quilt marking. If there is an Amish legacy to modern quiltmakers, it is an enduring inferiority complex and an obsession with perfectly matching borders and corners.

I understand that quilters often feel unsure of their ability to mark a quilt for quilting. The chapter headings of this book are taken from my students' most common questions. Many students come to the quilt marking class with quilt tops they've made in other classes. The simple directive to "Quilt as desired" had done nothing to build their confidence, and they had come to a complete halt in the quiltmaking process. What a shame! These are the people who want to enjoy quilting as much as they enjoyed making the quilt top. So, for these students who love to stitch and want to get on with finishing their quilts, I wrote this book.

The English quilt below was made in 1927 as a wedding gift, but the bride stored the quilt in a trunk. It eventually surfaced at her estate sale and was purchased by the present owner. The quilt displays the Northumberland style of quilt marking, and may have been marked by master quilt marker Elizabeth Sanderson. The blue pencil markings are still visible.

One-quarter of a twentieth century white-on-white wholecloth quilt. From the collection of Barbara Chainey.

Quilting is the bones of the quilt. All those stitches are what hold the top, batting, and backing together. The quality and quantity of the quilting will be a major factor in determining the longevity of your quilt. I have seen quilts 150 or more years old still held together by their quilting stitches. Calicoes may fade, binding fray to threads, and batting flatten to nothing, but the power of those little stitches still holds the quilt together.

Although the fabrics used in the top of the quilt below are almost completely worn away, the excellent quilting stitches still keep it together. The quilt was treasured in spite of its frail condition. According to family members, an ancestor–a boy at the time–deserted from the Confederate army and was hidden in a pile of quilts, including this one, in the attic of the family home.

Besides holding the layers of the quilt together, quilting serves an important artistic purpose. Unlike paint, applied to only one side of an artist's canvas, quilting stitches create a second surface on the back of the quilt. Quilts are two-sided works of art.

Quilt Backings and Battings

As much as they could afford to be, quiltmakers of old were more conscious than we are today of the backings of their quilts. While utility quilt backings were often pieced from any plentiful fabric, the backings of "good" quilts were pieced from fabrics that would showcase the quilting.

It was not uncommon for a nineteenth century quiltmaker to turn her quilts over seasonally. The lighter side of the quilt was the summer side and the darker was the winter side. This practice not only rotated the wear on the quilts, it changed the entire look of the bedroom. When all-white quilts were the rage in the mid-nineteenth century, many quilters turned over their pieced or appliqué quilts to display the stitching against the white backing.

In general, quilting is to a quilt backing what a brocade weave is to fabric—it adds light, shadow, and dimension. On the top of the quilt it can accentuate the geometry of a pieced pattern. When an appliqué quilt is complimented by lots of background quilting, the appliqué shapes stand out more.

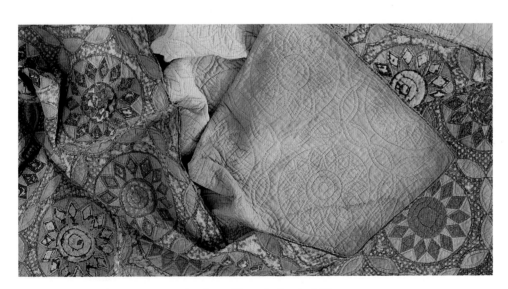

Unknown Pieced Pattern, c. 1860, from Blount's Creek, NC.
Gift of Carmella Hollis to the author.

Welsh Framed Center Diamond Quilt. 90" x 92". Pieced of silk and silk-wool fabrics in subtle colors, this quilt illustrates the link between Welsh and Amish quilts. It is dated 1818 in quilting stitches in the first frame below the diamond as shown in the detail below. Collection of Ardis and Robert James.

The backing fabric is a slightly glazed butternut brown cotton, similar to lining fabric used in clothing of the time. The quilting stitches are dark brown thread, and the complexity of the quilting designs clearly illustrates that quilting was valued in and of itself.

When the quilting design is not related to the quilt's construction the result can be both unexpected and delightful. The backing then presents a totally new composition.

The depth of the batting, called the loft, determines how dominant the stitches look in the overall effect of the quilt. Cotton batting, the choice of most American quiltmakers, could be purchased by the early 1900s in a uniform flat sheet rolled within a paper wrapping. Until that time, quiltmakers carded their own batting and could decide on the preferred weight for their quilts. Utility quilts often had thick battings, while good quilts, which displayed the quiltmaker's skill with a needle, were made with very

thin batting. Wool was also used for batting, but it was never as popular in America as it was in England.

In order to emphasize the visual relief—that interplay of light and shadow resulting from the stitches sinking into the batting—the marking of the quilt designs needed to be thought through. While utility quilts were quilted in simple designs, heirloom quilts were lavished with fancy designs and lots of background quilting. The quilt marker, who may or may not have been the maker of the quilt top, took pride in her marking going unnoticed. It was the stitching that followed her directives that garnered the glory.

Mexican Rose Quilt, c. 1850. Notice the exquisite background quilting. Collection of Patricia Cox.

Styles of Quilt Marking

While there are as many styles of quilt marking as there are quiltmakers, the following are the most common approaches.

Quilting that Follows the Piecing. This style has two variations: in-the-ditch quilting and by-the-piece quilting. In-the-ditch means the quilter quilts as near as possible to the seams of the patchwork. In-the-ditch quilting is hardly noticeable from the top of the quilt, and produces a perfect echo of the seam lines on the back of the quilt. By-the-piece quilting is also dictated by the seams, but the quilter stitches 1/4 inch inside or outside the shapes of the patchwork.

By-the-piece quilting got its big boost when newspaper quilting advice columns in the 1930s suggested their readers quilt this way. Conveniently, by-the-piece quilting avoids the fabric under each seam and is thus easier to quilt. The two most common methods for marking by-the-piece quilting is by chalking a line 1/4 inch from the seams with the aid of a ruler, or using 1/4" quilters' masking tape.

The back of the crib quilt—a creative combination of old Snail's Trail and Road to California blocks—indicates it was quilted in the by-the-piece style 1/4 inch from the seams of the pieced blocks. Crosshatching was marked over the border of "cheater patchwork."

Plain Quilting. A crosshatching or grid design is an example of "plain quilting." Old-time quilters working on a full-size quilt frame marked plain quilting by snapping long strings covered with chalk dust over the surface of the quilt. A vertical or horizontal grid would be marked by sighting along the seams of the blocks or by aligning the strings with points marked at even intervals on the frame itself. More often the chalked string method was used to mark diagonal crosshatching. Two people stood at opposite corners of the quilt frame and stretched between them a chalk-dusted string along the quilt's surface. When the string was in the desired position over the quilt, one person leaned forward, lifted up the taut string, and "snapped" it by quickly letting it loose. The string bounced off the quilt and left a chalked line corner to corner. Then they moved to the

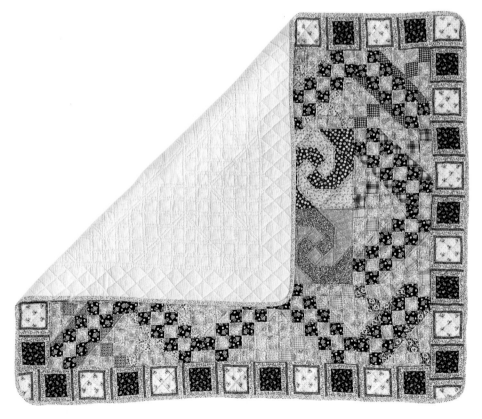

Recently Quilted Crib Quilt.
42" x 51". Collection of the author.

remaining opposite corners and repeated the process to mark a large "X" across the quilt. Additional lines were snapped with the string or marked with the aid of a yardstick and chalk.

Fancy Quilting. The designs applied to a quilt top with the aid of templates or stencils are collectively known as "fancy quilting." Among the best-known are the feather and cable designs. Quilts are rarely marked exclusively with fancy designs, however, as this has a tendency to make the batting mound up between the designs. When the batting is puffy polyester, the designs look as though they were stamped on the quilt. The unquilted areas of the quilt are a liability, where the unsecured batting will likely pull apart with use.

Fancy quilting is at its best when combined with lots of plain quilting. Plain quilting becomes the background to the designs. The fancy quilting thus highlights the dimensionality of the quilt's surface and lifts the designs up to view. The plain background quilting, especially when executed in close lines, flattens the quilt's surface, making for an almost corduroy effect.

Classic Revival: Alex's Quilt. 96" square. A group quilt made under the direction of Elly Sienkiewicz. Collection of Elly Sienkiewicz.

Country Quilting. This variation of all-over quilting has more than one name. In addition to country quilting, it was called shell quilting, wave quilting, elbow quilting, and fan quilting. It was regionally known as Baptist Fan, Methodist Fan, or even Lutheran Fan, probably depending on the church the quilter attended.

Country quilting was marked with minimal tools. The templates for the arcs were dinner plates, saucers, or cups that the quiltmaker traced around. Or the quilt was marked after it was in the frame with a primitive compass made from a length of string knotted at even intervals. The string was held at the side of the frame with the marker's thumb pressed down on one of the string's knots. A piece of white chalk was tied to the string's end. With the string taut and level at the quilt's surface, the marker set the chalk on the side of the frame and then traced a large arc on the quilt top. The marker repositioned the string compass at the next knot, drew a smaller arc within the first, and continued in this manner until the quilt was marked.

When you look at an old quilt quilted in this manner, you can tell if the quilter worked alone or with help.

The all-over waves of quilting in the quilt opposite indicate that it was most likely quilted in a traditional floor frame that rolled the quilt under as its sides were completed. A single quilter marked all her arcs in one direction, marking the design away from where she sat and stitched. Two or more quilters worked from both sides of the frame and produced opposing billows of cloud shapes that met in the middle. A skilled quilter often marked a single arc with a string compass and judged the following arcs by eye as she quilted. Some did away with the string compass altogether and simply set an elbow on the edge of the quilt frame, chalk in hand, and used the distance from elbow to hand as the sweep of the arcs they marked.

Country quilting in these undulating waves is especially attractive on scrap or string quilts. The effect is classic and introduces a contrasting surface texture to the straight lines of the piecing. Some stencils in fan patterns are also available, but the size of the arcs is limited. When marked the old-fashioned way, any size fan is possible.

Detail of Red Welsh Whole-Cloth Quilt. Photo of full quilt on page 30.

New York Beauty variation, c. 1900. 80" square. Found in
Burlington, NC. From the collection of Lynn and Will Gorges.

Although I would love to believe that folks think about what they will quilt on their tops before the top is complete, the fact is that most quilters tend to first make their tops and then think about how to mark and quilt the piece after the top is finished. After the exhilarating rush of piecing the top, or perhaps the opposite scenario—the long saga of appliqué—the average quilter tends to come to a halt in the quiltmaking process. Take advantage of this time to step back and look at the quilt top as objectively as possible. Ask yourself some questions.

Looking at the Quilt Top from a Distance

Find a place to hang your quilt top where you can see it full length. If not on a wall (the ideal viewing position), then vacuum the living room rug, shut the dog or cat outdoors, and spread the top out on the floor. The next-best option is to spread it over a bed. Perhaps for the first time you will be seeing your quilt top as a large work of art. Now ask yourself:

◆ What style of quilt top is this?
◆ What type of quilting would compliment this quilt top?
◆ How much time am I willing to spend quilting this top?

Answers to these questions are often compromises.

What Style Is It?

If your quilt top is in a recognizable style, such as an old-fashioned scrap quilt, look at other scrap quilts with the same feeling. Do you want your quilt to look as though it was quilted in the nineteenth century? If so, you'll use a flat batting (cotton is my choice), thread in a basic color (white, tan, brown, or navy), and then mark a design that imitates the stitching on older quilts. You can also save designs from antique quilts; see "Preserving a Design from an Old Quilt." On old quilts, you will seldom see quilting more than three or four inches apart since quilters were quite practical and wanted their quilts to stand up to use and wear.

In a simple scrap quilt, quilting can be marked in diagonal lines across the quilt, creating a diamond grid effect. This diagonal quilting is very strong. It actually replicates, on a larger scale, the steps of darning. When you darn (mend holes), stitches are made vertically, then horizontally, and finally diagonally in both directions. A darned fabric is stronger than the original fabric, and diagonal quilting often ensured an old quilt's survival. It's also a good choice for a modern quilt that will see a lot of use.

Inspired by Barbara Johanna's *Crystal Piecing* book, Rita Blaugher designed her scrap quilt of right triangles and then machine quilted diagonal lines across the blocks. This simple approach to quilting makes the quilt very strong while at the same time the lines of quilting do not distract from the sparkling colors and diverse fabrics in the quilt.

Detail from Modern Scrap Quilt. Collection of Rita Blaugher.

If your quilt has a real country down-home feeling, you should look at scrap quilts from the South. Instead of straight-line quilting, these often feature all-over quilting in large waves.

After you've determined the style of your top, you can either do research into the quilting done on antique quilts, or go off on your own and use modern tools to create an individual style as you mark.

Seams Are Not Fences

Some quilting texts place a lot of emphasis on laying out your quilting design to avoid having to stitch over seams. While I sympathize a little with that notion, it also severely limits the creativity of the quilter. A seam represents only a fractionally longer stitch than the stitch size the quilter regularly takes. In other words, it's no big deal. Quilt judges will not mark a quilter down for that minute variation in stitch size. And if the quilting is interesting and well thought out, quilting across the seams may net you admiration from a judge.

The muslin backing on the quilt below displays a quartet of cotton bolls. The cotton is depicted in white thread, while the stem ends of the bolls are in brown thread. Repeated ripples of quilting flow across the triple borders. The distinctive color scheme of this quilt—golden orange, Prussian blue, and oxblood brown—mark it as a North Carolina quilt.

Contrast the Quilting with the Top Construction

When you choose fabrics, they should coordinate, but when selecting a quilting motif you should contrast it with the style of the quilt top to showcase both the top construction and the quilting. A pieced quilt with lots of little angles usually benefits from some curved-line quilting. An appliqué quilt, with curves already in the design of the quilt top, looks good with straight-line quilting. A quilt that has straight-line piecing but which stylistically produces a curved effect, such as a bargello quilt, looks better

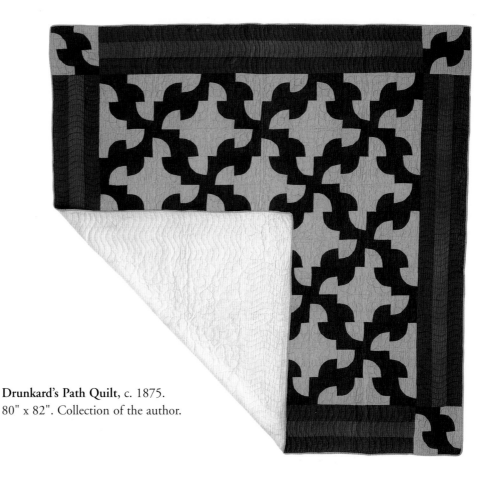

Drunkard's Path Quilt, c. 1875.
80" x 82". Collection of the author.

quilted with curves that echo the waves of color in the quilt top. Quilts with alternating plain blocks offer the opportunity for both plain quilting and fancy designs.

In the Opinion of the Professionals

Some well-known quilting teachers and authors are known for their styles of quiltmaking. I asked some of my friends in the quilt world to offer their opinions on quilting in general so you could see what "the pros" do when they quilt.

The Artistic Impact of Quilting. Alexandra Capadalis Dupré, Fairfield Fashion designer and author of *Men's Vests*, admits she is infatuated with the lavish hand quilting of antique quilts. "It adds dimension, reflects light, and enhances the tactile quality of the quilt. Whether it is done by hand or machine, I dote on every stitch. The quilting process is an intimate dialogue between the quilt and myself. Stitch by stitch, it transforms the two-dimensional design into a richly embellished surface. The stitches bind my heart and soul to the quilt. Quilting is the essential element that elevates the quilt to an artistic expression from within me."

She insisted that the border quilting on this original appliqué quilt had to be her own design, and finally settled on dozens of silhouettes of her own hands.

My Own Folk Art by Alexandra Capadalis Dupré. 80" square. Collection of the maker.

Charm Quilts. Beth Donaldson, author of *Charm Quilts*, advises that dazzling feats of quilting are wasted on busy, colorful charm quilts. She favors easy-to-mark straight-line quilting that takes its cue from the shape of the single charm template used in the quilt. For instance, when a half-hexagon is the template, two straight lines per template create a very effective six-pointed star quilting design. She also points out that all-over quilting designs, such as clamshells and fans, work well on charm quilts.

Miniature Quilts. Nancy Johnson-Srebro, well known for her miniature masterpieces, says, "Sometimes with miniature quilts, less is more. Too much quilting can distort tiny quilts. I often quilt in-the-ditch on pieced blocks, but when it comes to borders, a petite cable is really nice. I also like the effect of 'washboard quilting', lines of stitching 1/4" apart that I quilt on either side of 1/4" wide masking tape."

Scrap Quilts. Judy Martin, known for her pieced blocks and her classic book *Scrap Quilts*, likes quilting in flowing curves inspired by nature. She loves originality in quilting designs, especially those that relate to the blocks rather than merely echoing them. She prefers traditional style hand quilting in large plain areas, but advocates machine quilting on uniformly pieced quilts in order to more easily move across the seams with designs linking one block to another.

A Variation on Straight-Line Quilting. Mary Mashuta is a teacher, the author of *Stripes in Quilts*, and a Fairfield Fashion designer. She uses a two-step process for machine quilting. All seams are stitched in the ditch with monofilament thread, following a block grid by stitching along piecing seams. Then she makes the quilt "come alive" with larger stitching that the viewer will notice. These stitching lines emphasize and enhance the block structure and are in rayon or metallic thread. To create her designs she works parallel to the edges or uses midpoints to create starting points for new lines. Since everything is already held in place by the initial grid, she does not have to quilt every seam.

Quilts Using Plaids and Ethnic Prints. Roberta Horton, author of *Plaids and Stripes* and the designer of an extensive line of plaid cotton fabrics, often quilts along the pattern lines of the plaids. She relates, "I let the fabric tell me how to quilt," and applies that philosophy to unusual ethnic prints as well as her trademark plaids. In order to preview her quilting and ensure she will quilt all areas of the quilt evenly, she draws the quilting lines on clear acetate that she pins over the quilt top as it hangs on her design wall. Then she lays the acetate over white paper and checks to see that the quilting is well distributed over the surface of the quilt. Often she tries multiple quilting designs before deciding what to quilt. If her top is being quilted by someone else, the acetate overlay serves as a guide.

"No More Monkeys Jumpin' On the Bed" features plaid fabrics by Roberta Horton. As shown in the detail below, straight lines of quilting, when aligned with the weave of the plaids, are barely visible, but diagonal lines across the plaids show up well. Full quilt on page 71.

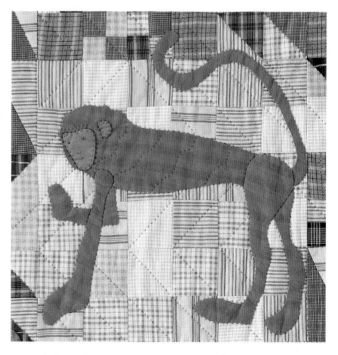

Detail from "No More Monkeys Jumpin' On the Bed" by Alexandra Capadalis Dupré. Collection of the maker.

Machine Quilting. Harriet Hargrave, who taught most of us to machine quilt, believes "the more quilting, the better!" She cautions machine quilters to quilt evenly over the quilt and puts no credence in quilt batting manufacturers' claims that batting can be quilted as far as six to eight inches apart. She thinks three inches apart is still the best guideline for work that will stand the test of time. Harriet hopes more people will continue making larger quilts because, she claims, "There is magic in making a bed quilt and then wrapping it around you."

Signature Quilts. Susan McKelvey is the author of numerous books on color and is also known for her expertise in the treatment of writing on quilts. She calls herself a "lazy marker" since she prefers to mark a close grid, using a ruler, on her quilts. She uses a #2 pencil on light color fabrics and a silver pencil on dark fabrics. All pencil lines are hidden by the quilting stitches.

Detail from "Two For Two" by Pepper Cory and Susan McKelvey. The sentiment in the center of this Memory Block is not obscured by the quilting stitches. Collection of the author.

Susan advocates that one should quilt as heavily on inked (signed) blocks as the rest of the quilt, but advises students not to quilt over the signatures since it would obscure the writing. Rather she quilts up to the signature, and then "travels" the needle (pushes it through the batting) to emerge on another line of quilting.

Appliqué Quilts. Jeana Kimball, designer of numerous patterns and appliqué books, says she pays attention to old quilts and imitates their quilting style. Often she brings a grid right up to the edges of her appliquéd shapes but usually does not outline the shapes. Then she picks some detail within the appliqué and quilts that. For example, in a floral appliqué, she might quilt the center of the flower or outline the veins in the leaves. When it comes to borders, Jeana often changes designs from what she used in the blocks, imitating a nineteenth century quilting format. Her modern quilts are as closely and finely quilted as antique quilts.

Celtic Style Appliqué. Philomena Durcan, who introduced Celtic appliqué to the quilt world almost twenty years ago, says the interlacings of Celtic designs are visually stabilized by 1/2" or 1" grid quilting.

This is reminiscent of iron fences or the panes in stained-glass windows. After she completes her quilt top, she places vellum graph paper over the pattern and designs the quilting. Her favorite marking tools are a mechanical pencil or a #3 hard lead pencil for light fabrics, and a gray or white erasable Roxanne pencil for dark fabrics. Philomena's last word on marking is "always use a light touch."

Colourwash or Watercolor Quilts. Deirdre Amsden of England brought an impressionistic palette to patchwork when she invented colourwash, also called watercolor, quilts. She relates, "This technique is about blending fabrics into washes of colour. Unlike the visible seams of traditional patchwork, I aim to make seams disappear, and quilting, especially across the seams, helps to disguise them. I believe quilting is an integral part of the colourwash concept." Deirdre confirms her quilting design by pinning tracing paper over the finished quilt top and drawing the quilting, complete with colored pencil in the colors of her quilting threads, on the tracing paper overlay.

Baltimore-Style Appliqué Quilts. Elly Sienkiewicz, who has made Baltimore-style appliqué her life's work, says, "Just as a Baltimore-style quilt is an album of appliqué designs, it can also be an album of quilting designs. I like to see different styles of background quilting, such as chevrons in one block and clamshells in another, within the same quilt." Sometimes Elly designs representational quilting motifs for personal reasons. "I wanted something special quilted in a favorite block, so I marked oak leaves and acorns, symbols of remembrance, around the applique."

I hope that some of the opinions offered by these well-known quilt designers and teachers will be of help to you as you choose what to mark on your own quilts. I cannot resist adding my own comments.

Amish Baskets by Pepper Cory, quilted by Gail Hill. 37" square. The pieced block, the colors, and the quilting designs of this quilt are based on early twentieth-century Amish quilts from Indiana and Ohio. "Railroad tracks" quilting crosses the basket blocks. Collection of the author.

Detail of Block from "Classic Revival: Alex's Album". Acorns and oak leaves add extra texture to this delightful block. Full quilt on page 11.

In general, I am in favor of dense quilting on a piece. The minute scale of stitching, whether by hand or machine, dictates that it must be repeated generously over the whole quilt surface. I like the contrast between curves and straight lines. When I see a busy, hard-to-see print marked with a fancy quilting design, I feel sorry for the quiltmaker. I know how she struggled with marking that print and how stitching that design must have strained her eyesight. On a busy print, I'd rather see a simple grid than an intricate design.

I'm tired of stippling as the "let's get it done quick" solution. When scrawled all over a quilt it is repetitious and adds little to the quilt's overall effect. On the other hand, I love well-done stippling contrasted with fancy designs or executed in fancy colored threads.

I like to see original quilting designs, but I also approve of traditional designs on quilts obviously done in an antique style. I find it jarring to see an Amish type solid-color quilt with very non-Amish quilting designs.

Puffy polyester batting quilted in simplistic designs makes for a kind of "comforter-found-in-a-department-store" feeling. In other words, these quilts seem less original and more mass-produced. When you hand your quilt top over to a professional machine quilter, there is a difference between the hand-guided machine stitching, and the pre-programmed quilting of one repeated motif over the whole quilt. You and the professional quilter need to consult and make sure you're both in agreement as to what would look good on your quilt.

Some stores sell inexpensive quilts made overseas and represent these as equal to hand-made American quilts. While I'm not opposed to the sale of these decorator quilts, I am concerned that the few remaining American quilting bees that produce quilts for sale will be adversely affected by these inexpensive imports. If you are buying a quilt and want to be sure of its origins, check the quality and the quantity of its quilting. While patchwork and appliqué patterns can be easily duplicated and modern fabrics used to make these quilts, the real difference between imported and American quilts is often found in the stitching. An observant quilt buyer can recognize when quilting is sloppily done and stitches are uneven or too large. The choice of quilting designs, and whether the quilt was marked and quilted with care, is evidence of a developed craft and thus is difficult to emulate in a strictly commercial venue. If, as quiltmakers ourselves, we keep our standards high, our work will not be devalued in the future with mass-produced quilts. Just the opposite—our hand-made quilts will be more sought after and treasured.

49'er Fever. 78" square. The wave quilting is marked across the Log Cabin blocks. Made by Carolie Hensley for her husband Tom, a San Francisco 49'ers fan.

Survey of Tools Used to Mark Quilting

This is not an endorsement of any particular products on the market. Specific brand names will be listed under Resources. Think of this as a checklist of all the common markers and tools used to mark quilts; it's designed to help you make good choices for your particular quilt.

Markers

Lead Pencil. This is the traditional standby tool of most quilters. It shows on white or light-colored fabrics. My favorite is a mechanical lead pencil in a hard lead (#2.5 or #3) with a 0.5mm size lead. Why use a mechanical pencil rather than a writing pencil you can sharpen to a lethal point? Mechanical pencils last much longer when using stencils since the little metal sheath around the lead protects it as the pencil runs through the slots of the stencil. Besides, I'd much rather punch down a new bit of lead than run to the pencil sharpener every five minutes. Plus I think mechanical pencils are neater and less inclined to smudge. Pencils are still the first choice of most

quilters to mark light-color quilts. The other part of this tool, the one we forget about, is its eraser. Since a pencil's eraser is likely to run out long before its lead, you will need another backup eraser. Check out squishy gray-colored erasers, labeled "Fabric Eraser," sold in fabric and art supply stores. These work well on fabric.

Water Markers. These come in both the blue and purple variety, and their appeal is that the vivid colors show well on so many colors of fabric. The purple type was developed for the tailoring industry to mark buttonholes, etc. The manufacturers claim that it will self-erase within a 24-hour period as the humidity in the air dissolves the purple color. **If you live in any sort of humid climate, this is not the marker of choice for you.** You'll be re-marking your quilting design every three or four hours! The blue markers are longer-lived than the purple type, but unfortunately, there can be serious drawbacks to both of these markers.

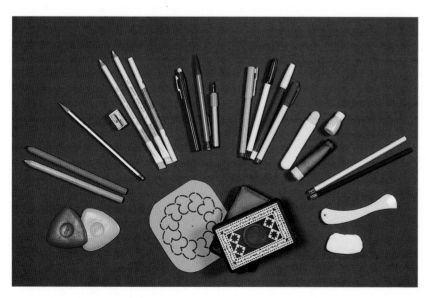

Common Marking Pencils and Tools.

Tools (left to right around the arc)
Tailor's chalks
Wooden pencils
Beryl silver pencil
Short cone sharpener for chalk pencils
Chalk pencils
Click-down eraser
Mechanical pencil
Graphite marker in metal holder
Blue water marker, purple "invisible"
  water marker
Blue water markers
Powder chalk wheel marker with refill bottle
Lipstick-shaped chalk wheel marker
Marking pencils
Hera marker
Soap sliver
In the center a stencil next to a box of
  blue pouncing powder with an
  eraser-like pounce pad

Few manufacturers have really tested their water markers or can tell you the ingredients in the ink. And neither the purple nor the blue water markers completely disappear from the fabric. When treated properly, the marks are not visible to us, but that does not mean they have actually lifted themselves from the fabric like magic. If you left the marks on the quilt without thorough washing, the blue ink might reappear as a ghostly brown line. It might even create tiny holes in the quilt top. Take the instructions on the label to heart. If it says, "Don't use this marker on red fabric because the ink might bond to the red dye and become permanent," believe it. Use cold water to take out the marks. Put a few ice cubes in your water spritzer to make sure it's cold.

White-on-White Whole-Cloth Quilt. 86" x 94". This masterpiece of American quilt marking dates from around 1820 and was found in Philadelphia, PA. Faint pencil marks are still visible. This is the only whole-cloth quilt I've seen in which the main motifs are birds. The lace-like borders add delicacy and grace to this large composition and the 1/2" crosshatching flattens the background so the viewer notices every detail of the fancy designs. From the collection of Patricia Cox.

Do not iron unwashed fabric that has been marked with a water marker, even if it looks as though you've gotten the marks out by spraying. Until that piece has been thoroughly washed—as in a clothes washer—it is still at risk for the reappearance of marks. All water markers should be washed according to the instructions that come on the back of the packaging. Don't throw that packaging away—keep it for reference. I wouldn't buy any water marker that did not come packaged with instructions—ignorance is an invitation to disaster.

Check the label of the soap you will use to wash the quilt. **Many detergents have ingredients that react with the marker ink.** Don't wait too long to wash the piece. Letting a quilt sit for a year with water marker on it is a bad idea. It's also not a good idea to re-mark designs with water marker several times. Each time you mark, the water marker soaks deeper into the batting, making it harder to eventually get out. Finally, don't store quilts that have been marked with these markers in a hot attic or other suspect storage space. Heat is the primary factor in reappearing marks.

Perhaps this sounds as if water markers are absolute no-no's for the cautious marker. Not so. More educated use is the objective here. Sometimes it can be really hard to see marks on certain colors and prints. The water markers have their place in the tool kit of every quilter. Follow these guidelines when using water markers and you should have good results:

- Make a test block using some of the leftover fabric from your quilt top. Mark a few lines to see if the water marker is visible on your fabrics and then wash it to see if it comes out completely.

- Try to mark as you come to the design area in the quilt rather than marking the whole top before quilting.

- Never get heat near water-marked designs.

- Follow washing directions to the letter.

- Never store a quilt that was marked with water marker in a hot room such as an attic.

Colored Pencils. Quilters have adopted these pencils for use on fabric. The colors quilters most commonly use are white, silver, and yellow: the silver has the best reputation. They are sharpened like lead pencils but should still be handled gently. **Mark the thinnest line you need to see to stitch.**

Chalk Pencils. These came from the tailoring and dressmaking industry and were developed with fabric use in mind. The centers of these are very soft and should not be sharpened in an ordinary pencil sharpener, especially not an electric sharpener. If you are sharpening chalk pencils in a sharpener intended for lead pencils, you might as well stick a dollar bill in the sharpener and grind away! **Chalk pencils need to be sharpened with a hand-held short cone sharpener that produces a squat cone point.** Many times a short cone sharpener comes packaged with the chalk pencils. If one did not come with your chalk pencil, go purchase an eyebrow pencil sharpener at the cosmetic counter of your local drugstore since the consistency of chalk pencils and make-up pencils is quite similar. The common size chalk pencil comes in white, yellow, pink, and blue. You can also find fat wooden pencils in red, green, and blue. Use a short cone sharpener for *all* chalk pencils. **A last word about the fragility of these pencils—never tap them on the desk or play with them like drumsticks.** The centers can break even up inside the pencil. I put mine back into the little plastic pouch they originally came in and lay it in my sewing box. Don't store them point side down inside a cup with a lot of other pencils as that also wears down the centers.

Soapstone Markers. These are found at quilt stores and make a thin, pale gray line. Keep the soapstone to a sharp point by sharpening it in a metal crank type sharpener and maintain a point by scraping the point on sandpaper. After a little while, soapstone markers develop a hard-thin surface formed by contact with air and our hands. Re-sharpen the marker before using it. I have never heard of anyone having trouble getting soapstone marks out of their quilt.

Graphite Markers. These are relatively new on the market and have a metal holder similar to soapstone markers. This is the same substance as pencil lead, but without oil. They usually wash out easily, but remember that marking a thin line is the best policy.

Chalk Dusters, also called Pounce Pads. These were originally carpenters' tools and are still used in woodworking and construction today. Powdered chalk, either blue or white, is held in a soft fabric bag. The bag is then bounced ("pounced") up and down to dust some of the chalk on the desired spot, such as the holes in a paper pattern or the slots of a quilt stencil. The chalk marks on fabric are quite temporary and only remain if they are undisturbed. Even as you quilt a chalk-dusted design it seems to disappear. **Obviously, this is not the tool to use to mark designs that you won't be quilting right away.** First used in the nineteenth century, pounce pads made a comeback in the 1930s when batting companies recommended them for use with perforated paper quilting patterns. The white chalk dust was mixed with powdered fabric bluing and produced a nice sky-blue color chalk. The bluing was helpful when the quilt was washed as it promoted getting the marks out easily. Now a modern pounce pad that resembles a chalkboard eraser is found in quilt stores.

I have heard anecdotal accounts of chalk or flour being mixed with cinnamon to make a tan or brown dust that was used to mark white or light-colored quilts, but I cannot site a true historical account of this practice. Cinnamon was and still is a costly spice. I doubt the thrifty housewife would have used it to mark her quilts! However, what might be mistaken for cinnamon marks on an antique quilt could be red chalk since carpenters' pounce pads also came in that color.

Chalk Wheel Markers. These come in three basic shapes: a heart-shaped plastic holder with the wheel at the point of the heart, a lipstick-shaped marker which has a see-through plastic cover over the wheel end, and a slim stick-shaped marker. Invented for use in the tailoring and dressmaking industry, the powdered chalk is lightly dispensed as the little metal wheel rolls over the fabric. These chalk marks stay only a short time, but they are ideal for marking a simple design you're going to quilt immediately. I use chalk wheel markers primarily for marking soon-to-be-quilted designs and for marking registration lines on a quilt top before marking with stencils. They come in white, blue, yellow, and pink. The white marker is the most useful for marking on dark fabrics and it also seems to dust out the best. The only drawback to these markers is that you occasionally buy one in which the little wheel does not roll easily. Take it back to the store immediately and get a replacement. The reluctant wheel occurs most often in the heart-shaped markers.

Other Wheel Markers. A wheel marker, which looks like a spur with a wooden handle, is used to mark dressmaker patterns by rolling it across dressmakers' carbon paper. A few quilters use this wheel tool, properly called a rowel, to mark quilting designs. Generally the marks wash out easily if the quiltmaker washes the quilt soon after quilting. **Seamstress' carbon paper can get old, and when old paper is used, the marks can be difficult to wash out.**

Scratch Markers. A few old-fashioned quilters still scratch mark their quilts but the practice is not common today. The quilter takes a large embroidery needle with a dull point and scratches the design along the fabric where she wants to quilt. The beauty of this method is that there are no markings to worry about washing out later. **The drawback is that the scratch markings are harder to see and in humid weather don't last very long.**

Another tool used to scratch mark is the Japanese hera, a tool which is also finding favor with quilters as a foundation piecing presser. A butter knife or a letter opener with a dull blade are homemade substitutes for a hera. The hera works well for marking straight-line quilting rather than complex designs, and most quilters prefer to use the hera for marking after their quilt tops have been basted with batting and backing.

I recently made the acquaintance of the granddaughter of one of Mountain Mist's prize quilters. In the 1930s, ads for Mountain Mist batting featured quotes from Mrs. Blain Wilson, whose work was highly prized. Mrs. Wilson's granddaughter, Ann Manooch, said her grandmother was proud she always marked tops with the scratch marking method, or "laying off" as she called it, because she considered it superior to other marking methods.

Tailor's Chalk Triangles. These are sold wrapped in thin paper and boxed. Tailors mark alterations on men's suits with them but they can be used to mark quilting designs as well. The only ones I have seen are imported from Japan. Like all chalk markers their marks are only temporary.

Soap Slivers. These actually work rather well, and if you're into recycling, using them will make you feel quite righteous! When your white bath soap is down to a thin sliver, take it from its slimy dish and set it someplace to dry out. Leave it for at least two weeks. Gently scrape both sides of the sliver on sandpaper to make nice thin edges and then use it as you would the chalk markers. Obviously, soap slivers work best on dark color fabrics and wash out easily. **Avoid soaps with lots of moisturizers in them and opt for the white soap that's 99.9% pure and floats.**

The Difference between Templates and Stencils

Before I list the objects used as patterns for quilt marking, let me explain the difference between a template and a stencil. A template is any pattern created by marking around a shape, while a stencil is a pattern through which the design is transferred. A template can be any shape but a stencil is distinguished by the slits cut in the surface. Too often these terms are confused.

The subject of quilting stencils is discussed at length in Chapter 6, Getting the Most from Your Quilting Stencil.

Found-Object Templates. A creative quilt marker does not have to look any further than her kitchen for inspiration. The plates, cups, and saucers of her dishes provide a handy array of circular shapes she can use in devising designs for quilting. Cookie cutters in familiar shapes such as stars and hearts could also do double duty as quilting templates. The name of one quilting design of interlocking rings is the Wineglass, revealing its humble household origin.

Commercially Available and Found Object Quilt Marking Templates.

I have seen a few nineteenth century quilts with life-like leaves quilted in them. Perhaps the quilter collected the leaves, pinned them to the surface of the quilt, and quilted around them. I've also seen the quilted outline of a pair of scissors. Maybe those were her own scissors lying on the quilt as it was stretched in the frame and the quilter decided to memorialize them. The most poignant design I remember seeing in a quilt was the outline of two hands. One was large (the quilter's?) and one was small—perhaps the outline of her child's hand.

Tin Templates. Some lucky quilters possessed their own tin quilting templates. These were not commercially available in the nineteenth century but rather made for them by husbands and sweethearts. While a few tin templates survive in museum or private collections, the majority of our quilting ancestors made their own templates from paper or recycled cardboard cut from boxes or calendars.

Paper Patterns. Paper patterns of quilting designs are still being produced today. Few give the 1930s directions to perforate and then dust the design onto the quilt with chalk. Now full-size paper patterns for whole-cloth quilts are printed on sheets of paper one-quarter the size of the quilt. These patterns are pinned underneath the white or light-colored fabric. The designs show through so they can be traced onto the quilt. When a quarter of the quilt is completely marked the quilter moves the top and continues marking until the full design is transferred.

Morman quilters often transfer the paper designs first to an old sheet and mark the designs with black permanent pen. The sheet is then laid under the top and the easy-to-see design transferred to the quilt top.

Peel-Away Paper Templates. You can make your own peel-away templates by drawing quilting designs on paper and then lightly spraying an adhesive called mounting spray on the back of the paper. This is available at art supply stores. The slightly tacky back allows you to position the paper template on the quilt and to quilt around the shape. After some use, the paper template will need to have more spray applied. Contact paper can also be used for peel-away quilting templates. Draw on the top surface of the contact paper and cut out the shape. Peel away the backing and position the template on the quilt and quilt around it. Whenever using templates with a sticky surface, the best policy is minimal contact with the fabric. **Don't leave them on the quilt for long in case they leave a sticky residue you'll have to get out later.**

Early Homemade Templates of Paper and Buckram. The Amish cut templates from bonnet buckram, a stiff net-like fabric used to give shape to their bonnets.

Templates such as these were either pinned directly to the quilt and then quilted around or were models for making more permanent templates.

Amish Paper Quilting Templates. c. 1900, From Pennsylvania. From the author's collection.

They also used any spare paper for templates. I found templates at an Amish auction made from flattened cereal boxes, old letters, postcards, the backs of auction posters, and brown paper grocery bags.

New Quilting Templates. Quilting templates are still available today. A set of plastic feather shapes in graduated sizes can help fill in an awkward space at the corner of a quilt or make a feather wreath in a size you can't find in a commercial stencil. Metal feathering templates, in both fat and elongated variations, are also manufactured, along with some metal cable templates. While the number of metal templates is limited and they are more expensive than their plastic counterparts, they are quite useful to the designer who wants to create new quilting designs.

Tear-Away Patterns for Quilting. Paper patterns for continuous-line quilting are popular with machine quilters. The directions state that hand quilters can also use them if they take the time to cut through the bridges in the paper stencils as they quilt. Follow all pattern specifications (stitch length, etc.) for the best results. You can also use old dress-pattern tissue or tracing paper and draw your own quilting designs for tear-away patterns.

There are several carageenan-based (seaweed) papers used for marking cutwork embroidery that quilters have found useful for marking machine quilting. The quilter draws her design, pins the paper to the quilt, machine sews, and then rinses the quilted area to dissolve the paper.

Marking Tape. Different widths of masking tape can be used to mark straight-line quilting. You use the tape as a guide when quilting. The smallest is a 1/8" tape, found in auto-detailing stores. Other widths of masking tape are available in hardware stores. I prefer painter's masking tape, which is the slightest bit less sticky than other masking tape. I am also careful to "de-stickify" tape first by laying it over the knee of my jeans and then applying it to the quilt. The extra fibers picked up from my jeans ensure the tape will not leave a residue.

When people have problems with tape marking, they generally have left the tape on for a long time. You should only tape mark the area of quilting you're going to do on any one day and be sure to take off the tape as soon as you've quilted that area of the quilt.

Rulers for Marking Straight-Line Quilting. There are so many rulers on the market today that the selection is staggering. For marking straight-line quilting, I think the see-through plastic rulers normally used for rotary cutting are excellent. The various acrylic square rulers, ranging in size from 4" square to 16 1/2" square, are also useful. To mark lines on the diagonal (at a 45-degree angle), use a rotary ruler that has the 45-degree lines on it. Do not confuse the 45-degree with the 60-degree lines found on the ruler—put a piece of masking tape over those so you won't get confused about the correct angle when marking. A carpenter's square is also useful for marking 45-degree lines.

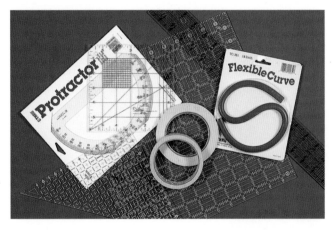

Other Marking Tools. (Lower left and across) Rotary cutting triangle tool (yellow printing), small rotary square (red printing), oversize protractor, two different widths of masking tape, flexible rubber curve, large rotary cutting square (yellow printing), rotary cutting ruler (blue printing).

Flexible Curve for Marking Curved Lines. This handy tool is found at office and art supply stores. Made from bendable rubber enclosing a metal inner strand, the flexible curve can be manipulated into any curve you like. It keeps its shape and can be used to mark multiple curves.

Light Table. A light table is a useful tool for transferring designs onto fabrics. Essentially a box topped with a piece of glass, a lightbulb inside the box illuminates the glass surface. To trace a paper quilting design the quilter tapes it to the box and lays the fabric over it. When the light is turned on the design shows through the fabric and you can then see and mark the design. Light tables are available by mail order and in art supply stores.

If you have a dining table with leaves, you can separate the leaves and lay a large pane of glass or plexiglass across the gap. If you carve your own quilt stencils (see Chapter 8) you probably have a glass pane of the appropriate size. Place a lamp (minus shade) on the floor below the table. Tape your paper design to the glass, turn on the lamp, and trace the design onto the fabric. Glass-topped coffee tables combined with a small lamp also work for marking.

Another possibility is to tape the design to a window on a sunny day. Tape the quilt top over it and trace the design. While this works well with smaller quilts, it is awkward with large quilts as you must move and re-tape the quilt top several times.

With this survey the majority of quiltmakers should be able to find several satisfactory marking tools. The fact is that we are always evolving in our quilting and there are so many products used to mark quilts that I hear about new ones all the time. No single method of marking or one particular tool will fill all our marking needs all the time.

As you become more confident marking quilts, you'll find you have to be flexible in your methods and timing. No one marker and no one tool will do the marking job every time. Our eyesight can change with time, and we might find that the very thin pencil line we used to mark is not as visible as it once was. We can deal with some of the effects of aging eyesight by analyzing our quilting habits.

Where We Work

We get so used to sitting in one chair and working by the light of one lamp that we don't realize we're straining our eyes. Not until we get a headache or unconsciously start to avoid quilting—which we once loved—do we stop and think about how we mark and quilt our quilts. If you're having trouble seeing marking lines, this is the cue for a visit to the optometrist. Have your eyesight checked, and if you wear glasses, get the prescription checked against the results of the latest exam.

Maybe it's time to move the furniture a bit in your sewing nook. Is that overstuffed armchair really the best chair for quilting? Perhaps a cushy secretary's chair, with nice padding and good support, would be a better choice.

Look at the lighting where you quilt. Fluorescent lighting, especially from bulbs that have been in the fixtures a long time, is probably the worst lighting

Pacific Chain by Laurel Horton. 83" square. The well-known Irish Chain pattern is updated here with batik and ikat fabrics. Traditional cross-hatching marked on the checker-board blocks meets a modern swirl design as it spirals over the alternate blocks. Collection of the maker.

for quilting. Replace some of the fluorescent tubes with full-spectrum tubes. This will balance the cool effect of fluorescent light and also make fabrics show their true color. Ask yourself if you can't get more lighting into your quilting nest. Many people find quilting near a window in natural daylight, especially in the morning, is the best lighting solution.

How We Mark Our Quilts

If you're used to picking up a pencil to mark quilt tops for quilting, one day you'll find to your dismay that pencil lines don't show on gray fabric, that they also don't show on many busy prints, and in short, that your latest project requires a new marking tool. If you've read this far, you know there are a lot of markers out there and one of them, or perhaps several of them if the quilt features a variety of fabrics, will do the job. As you first experimented in your quilting, it's time to try new tools and use them in different ways.

How You Can Prepare for Marking as You Sew the Quilt Top

As you assemble your quilt top, save a scrap of each fabric you use in the quilt. If you are really organized, cut a small square (3" is fine) of each fabric. Sew these squares together randomly into a larger block after completing the top. This will be the test patch for markers. It can also serve as a record of that quilt's fabrics, and turn into a coordinating pillow for the quilt.

Sort through your available markers and use several to test-mark quilting lines on your scrap. Look at the lines on the different fabrics. What can you see the best? Following the washing directions for the markers; do they wash out? [A caution here—if you're using water markers do not iron the patch at this point.] If you can see the marker lines to quilt and the lines wash out of the test patch, then you can safely use those markers to mark your quilt.

Use your test patch as a warm-up exercise for quilting the whole quilt. Machine quilters know the wis-

dom of practicing before starting to quilt a large project. They check out their machine's stitching and refamiliarize themselves with the motion of moving the quilt layers easily through the machine. Hand quilters will also find their stitches improve with a stint of pre-quilt practice.

Marking Has Timing

When all quilts were quilted on a full-size floor frame, marking was usually done when the quilt was in the frame. Since we now quilt in a variety of ways—on a traditional frame, in a hoop, or lap quilting without a frame—we can mark our quilts in a more step-by-step fashion. We can mark a block as we come to it. If we've thought through the marking, that leisurely attitude should pose no problems. It's usually at the borders and when marking background quilting that we start to lose confidence.

The border conundrum can be solved by making a paper model (see Chapter Eight). Marking background quilting is more easily accomplished with the quilt spread out full length. If possible, push two tables together (your church parish hall or quilt store classroom on a quiet day is an ideal spot) and lay the quilt out. With the use of rulers, masking tape, and stencils you can find a background design you can keep straight on the quilt. This is not the time to just "wing it," especially if your background quilting compliments fancy designs. Take your time.

Whole-Cloth Marking Is Different

An exception to marking as you go is the classic whole-cloth quilt. Since all the work is in the stitching, the whole thing must be marked before you begin to quilt. Depending on the marker you've used, you might have to re-mark part of a design occasionally if the markings have rubbed off with handling. I find when quilting a whole cloth that I like to quilt the fancy designs in an area and then go back and fill in with background quilting. Changing off from the fancy to the plain quilting keeps me from getting tired of the work. However, I would not quilt all the fancy designs in a whole cloth and then fill in all the background quilting afterwards. Quilt both the fancy designs and the background in the body of the quilt before moving out to the borders.

Whole-Cloth Quilts Today

If you've never seen a whole-cloth quilt before reading this book, they may strike you as incredibly formal and old-fashioned and obviously way above your head. I would like to encourage you to consider whole-cloth quilts again as a class in quilting self-improvement. A small-scale whole-cloth quilt will boost your quilting abilities as no other project can.

You will be able to trace your progress as your quilting improves. It's like skipping several grades in school—your quilting ability leaps forward dramatically.

Another tidbit about whole-cloth quilts is that they always get a lot of attention. People think of them as masterpiece quilts. There are so few made and entered at quilt shows that they almost always get a ribbon. So if you're yearning for quilt show fame and acclaim, make a whole cloth. There's not a lot of competition—yet.

Welsh Red Wool Whole-Cloth Quilt. 68" x 77". Made c. 1900-1925.
From the collection of Jane Lury, Labors of Love Antique Quilts.

We are lucky today that we have so many sources for quilting designs. Many companies manufacture stencils, and they can be found at fabric and quilting stores, at vendors' booths at quilt shows, in mail-order needlework catalogues, and on the Internet. Building a personal collection of favorite quilting stencils can be as useful to the quiltmaker as assembling a library of how-to books.

When faced with a selection of stencils, and with no particular project in mind, we can think of quilting stencils as designs that can be transferred exactly in their entirety or as parts of designs we can repeat and reassemble in different ways. When we're in search of a design for a particular size space or border, especially when time is a factor, we tend to be less open to the possibilities stencils represent. I encourage you to think of stencils as tools in your adventure of quilt marking.

The feather circle below with basket-weave center, punched from heavy cardstock paper, was manufactured and sold by Wurzburg's Department Store of Grand Rapids, Michigan in the 1920s and 30s.

Early Manufactured Quilting Stencil. From the collection of Ann Manooch.

A Selection of Block Designs.

The Fleur-de-Lis shown above (upper left) is a tear-away paper pattern. The blue stencil (upper right) is from Stencil House, the pink stencil (lower left) is by Pepper Cory for StenSource International, and the white butterfly stencil (lower right) is from Quilting Creations International.

Sometime when you don't care to stitch, get out your stencil collection, a pencil, and a roll of plain white drawing paper. Shelf paper, found in hardware and variety stores, is a good source for inexpensive paper.

As you play with the stencils, you will see sections of the designs can re-combine with others to create totally new patterns. Draw some of your new designs and make a note of which stencils you used. Keep that drawing in a file near your stencils. Congratulations! You're on your way to becoming a quilting designer.

Block Designs

Block designs are visually easy to comprehend. They depict some flower, geometric design, or outline of an object. The size of a block design is determined by the finished size of the quilt block. Look for block designs slightly smaller than the blocks you usually make. If the blocks you make are 12" square, then designs of 11" or 10" are good choices for your collection. Other little designs might fit in the small squares where sashing strips intersect. Their size depends on the width of your sashing. For instance, if you often make sashing strips 3" wide, designs of 2" or 2 1/2" would be appropriate.

Border Designs

The borders of quilts are traditionally where you expect to find fancy quilting designs. Perhaps that's because adding a border is the last time the quiltmaker can expand the size of the quilt top, and she needs quilting on the border to frame and visually finalize her work. Border stencils come in three forms: borders without corners, borders with corners, and sets of border and corner stencils. Think of fancy quilting on borders as being similar to the gilt on a frame around a painting. The frame is necessary to showcase the art but the gilt adds something special to the presentation.

Too often quiltmakers think that the seams of their borders define the only quiltable areas of the border. But some freethinking quilters mark border designs that encompass multiple borders. The best-known examples of encompassing border designs are seen in Amish quilts whose makers marked flowing feathers across two or three borders, or fat cables that wander across seams. This large-design-over-multiple-borders approach draws together diverse colors and widths of borders as it frames the quilt, and coincidentally, solves the problem of hunting for a different quilting design for every border.

Background Designs

These stencils are not as immediately recognizable or appealing as block designs. It might not even occur to some quilters to purchase them. I heard one woman who owned a quilt shop say, "Why should I stock stencils with crosshatching or clamshells? Folks just make their own with masking tape or by tracing around teacups!" While it's true some old-time quilters will insist on marking their background designs in a laborious fashion, stencils of background quilting patterns are priceless to the quiltmaker who values her time.

You might ask, "Why is background quilting important at all? Aren't people just going to look at the fancy blocks and corners? Why should I give any consideration to boring background quilting?" While I understand new quilters' impatience with the quilting process, an important point about background quilting is that lots of background quilting strengthens your quilt and makes your other beloved fancy designs much more noticeable. A well-quilted quilt withstands wear, cleaning, and time, and may well survive long enough to earn the status of family heirloom.

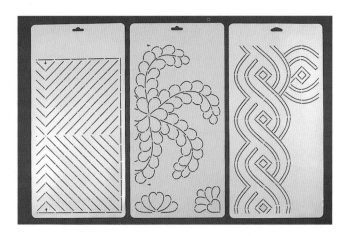

Background, Large Block and Border Stencils.

The background stencil (left) of converging diagonal lines looks wonderful quilted around a complex appliqué block. A whirling Princess Feather (center) is marked by marking the center rosette first and then adding the branches of feathers. Turn the stencil (following the arrows) to continue marking all the legs. The Amish border design (right) illustrates that sometimes you don't always have to turn the corner with a cable. This particular one looks corded when it's quilted due to the double lines.

The type of batting used also affects the quality of background quilting. While cotton batting used to be the most popular batting in the 1930s since it was commerically available and affordable, now polyester, cotton/polyester blends, and even wool batting can be found in quilt stores. Cotton is once again popular with quilters, both for machine and hand quilting, and a whole new generation is rediscovering the pleasure of quilting through airy wool batting. A puffy polyester batting sometimes needs more, not less, background quilting than many cotton battings. This is because with use and time, polyester batting tends to shift through the layers, and, unfortunately, the phenomenon we know as "bearding" (the polyester threads coming through the surface of the quilt) once started, never stops. More background quilting helps retard this gradual loss of batting fibers that we see in modern battings.

Other Stencils

A few large block designs are represented in half-stencils. It is usually obvious whether the stencil is either flipped over to complete the design or rotated, keeping the same side up, to complete the design. Stencils that must be manipulated to complete a

A Miniature Whole-Cloth Stencil. This popular stencil was inspired by whole-cloth quilts from the County Durham area of England. This book's cover quilt was marked with this stencil.

design have either small stickers of printed directions that explain how to do this or registration arrows cut in the stencil itself. If you have any doubt how to mark a large design and you have not yet purchased the stencil, ask the shop owner to show you how to use it. Or buy the stencil and take it home to experiment on paper. Perhaps you'll discover new ways to look at that design and so expand your marking possibilities.

New variations on these larger stencils are the sets of stencils that, when combined, result in whole-cloth quilt designs. Of course, creative quiltmakers have long designed their favorite motifs in the same quilt. Today whole-cloth quilts are being done in cotton, silk, and every color of the rainbow.

Another category of stencils is letter and number stencils. These are more often marketed as painting stencils than quilting stencils. Use them to mark your name, the name of the quilt's recipient, or the date of the quilt's completion. Some Midwestern Amish quiltmakers regularly use the four corners of the quilt to mark the quiltmakers' initials, the initials of the recipient of the quilt, the date the quilt was begun, and the date it was completed or given.

A few miscellaneous fancy designs, such as corner fill-in feathers, are also found in quilting shops. Don't forget that some painting stencils, if they are not too complex, can also serve for quilting.

Detail of Feather Quilting. This straight feather is quilted over a dark plaid fabric and it still shows up nicely. Quilting by Gail Hill. From the collection of the author.

The Most Popular Quilting Designs

I've conducted several informal surveys of what designs quilters like most, and invariably the hands-down favorite is feathers. There is something universally appealing about the sensuous curves of this classic motif, especially when set against straight-line background quilting.

When I reviewed the sales figures for different types of stencils, the best-selling ones were borders of all descriptions. Borders outsell all other designs by a three-to-one margin. Unfortunately, quilt shop owners are not aware of this fact. Like most quilters, they look through a stencil company's catalogue and are enchanted by the complete picture designs for blocks. That's why the shelves of a quilt shop's stencil department usually have gaps and the shops are always re-ordering. If I could give advice to someone just beginning a stencil collection, I would suggest they buy more borders than blocks, that when possible they should buy borders with corners already in the design, and that background stencils will save both time and their sanity.

Buying Stencils

When stencils are lined up on hooks at the quilt shop, the variety can be confusing. Try to remember the sizes of blocks and borders in your quilt—better yet, bring the quilt top with you to the shop. Spread the top out and audition the stencils on top of the fabric. If a stencil's design is not immediately evident to you, ask the shop owner if she would mind if you lightly traced the design on a piece of paper. Often any visual clutter clears up when you see the simple black lines on white paper. If the quilt is a repeated block pattern, set without sashing, marking a design across the blocks can be very intriguing. See Chapter 3, the section called In the Opinion of the Professionals, and Chapter 13, Quilting From the Judges' Point of View, for further thoughts on unconventional marking. Of course, if you mark designs across pieced blocks, you will have to deal with seams as you quilt, but then isn't art worth a little extra effort?

Amish Center Diamond. 16" square. Miniature quilt designed by Pepper Cory and quilted by Gail Hill.

Miniature whole-cloth quilt by Pepper Cory, quilted by Gail Hill. 16" x 18".

Diverse Opinions by Bets Ramsey. 64" x 37 1/2". The minimal piecing and appliqué in this quilt are accentuated by liberal lines of hand quilting. Photo by David B. Jenkins

Matching Borders and Corners

Perhaps because we admire the quilts of the Amish so much, we hold up as a standard of quilt marking the complex feathers and cables we see on these unique quilts. I used to wonder if Amish quiltmakers knew a secret, some passed down and treasured formula for making all their quilt borders fit. Then I had an opportunity to view Amish quilts up close and personal and saw rubbed out chalk marks. I realized they also struggled with matching borders and corners, with stretching their cable links, and with making the designs fit, just as we do today. What a relief! At least matching borders and corners wasn't a secret I hadn't yet earned the right to know! Obviously, there was hope for me. And there is for you, too.

But before taking the mystery out of matching borders and corners, let's consider that there are multiple ways to mark your quilt's borders. You may find one of the following a satisfactory solution. Here are ten ways to mark a border that do not involve matching.

Getting Around Matching Borders and Corners

◆ If overall designs, such as clamshell, waves, or a diagonal grid, are used in the body of the quilt, extend the design out over the borders. Here diagonal crosshatching extends into the borders.

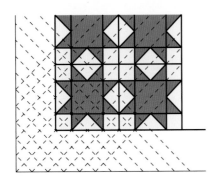

Diagonal Crosshatch

◆ Select a block design and mark it at even intervals along the border, thereby creating the illusion of a linear design by the repetition of the motif. The tails of the lovebirds below almost touch; as a result, the repeats create the illusion of a linear design.

Repeated blocks

◆ Mark a block design at the corners, then run a border design between the corners. A large heart anchors each corner while a vine stretches between the corners in the border below.

Block with border design

◆ Use selected block designs complimented by filler (background designs) that fill the space. In the border below, feather wreaths are complimented by lots of straight-line quilting.

Filler

◆ Use a draftsman's triangle or a carpenter's square (any large right-angle tool) to divide the border into right triangles. Start with a triangle at the border's midpoint, and then continue marking triangles out toward the corners. Mark off the corners as separate squares. The triangular marking can be used in two ways: The first approach considers the triangle area as the basic unit of the design and is completed by ruling parallel lines within the triangles in a basketweave fashion. Mark the corners as a series of L-shaped lines. The second way is to use the triangle areas as registration lines only, that is, as guides to marking other designs. Fill in the triangular spaces with another design. As shown below, a basketweave design emerges when the triangles are left as part of the design and accentuated with lines. In the second illlustration, triangles were chalked on the border first, and then the fancy curlicues were positioned within the triangles. The preliminary triangle marks were dusted off and only the fancy designs quilted.

Options with triangles

◆ Mark parallel diagonal lines at a 45-degree angle to the seam of the border and alternate these with thinner border designs also at a 45-degree angle. The space between the sets of lines and the border designs can vary according to personal preference. Here, a flowing border design is slanted at a 45-degree angle and interspersed with straight-line 45-degree angle lines.

◆ Using a circular tool such as an oversize protractor or a quilting hoop, mark the border in swags (half circles) and fill in the swags at their tangent points with smaller designs and background quilting. Unless you are lucky enough to have made a border evenly divisible by the diameter of your circular tool, the corner swag is not a full three-quarter circle but rather a more oval shape, and generally smaller than the swoop of the swags. A protractor or quilting hoop makes a good half-circle swag. At the top of the swag loops mark some crowning feathers or a flower, as shown below.

Swags

◆ Choose a right-angle design that branches in both directions and mark that in the four corners, working out toward the midpoints of the borders. Leave some area open at the midpoint and insert a second design there. This approach has the feeling of a formal monogram.

Midpoint design

◆ Select a block design and mark it at all four midpoints of the border. Then branch out toward the corners, leaving some open space at the 45-degree angle that delineates the corner. Using this method de-emphasizes the corners.

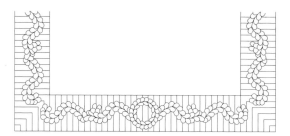

◆ Use a border design that fills the border space well and simply run the design off the ends of the quilt. The placement can be side borders marked first and then linked by the top and bottom design, or the designs can overlap, Log Cabin fashion, at each corner. The latter is, I think, the most graceful solution.

If these alternatives sound like cheating, they are not. Judges do not mark points off when these approaches are used to mark borders. Rather, in a competitive situation, judges admire a variety of methods for quilting borders, and will only criticize a quilt when its quilting style falters and is obviously not well-thought-out or properly applied. A little inventiveness, combined with confidence, goes a long way in the judging arena.

Matching Undulating Line Designs with Stencils

When marking an undulating (wavy) design such as a feather or a vine with leaves and flowers, remember the most important element is the line that defines the design. In the case of the feather, it's called the spine of the feather. Spines may be single or double lines. In the vine, the simple line of the vine, not its leaves or flowers, is the dominant element. When the spine of the feather is marked correctly, you can go back and use the stencil to mark the feathers on either side of the spine. If the line of the vine is to your liking, then it's time to use the stencil to add the details such as leaves and flowers.

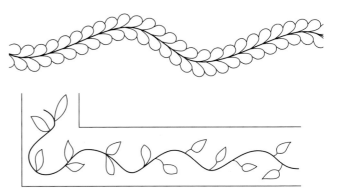

Europa Sampler. Appliqué by Bonnie Bus, other work by Pepper Cory. 41" square. This wall hanging was exhibited at Quilt Europa held in Brussels, Belgium. The intertwined feather and cable border beautifully frames the center blocks of this quilt. Collection of the author.

Corners

The four corners of the border designs should be alike. **One of the truths about border marking is that most people look at the corners first to see how the design turns the corner.** To visually tie the border design together, all the corners should be the same. It's only the intervals of the up and down waves that will vary somewhat on both the side borders and top and bottom borders, and that's only if you are marking a rectangular quilt. Mark the corners first and get them out of the way.

Before you say, "Well, I'll only make square quilts if matching designs on rectangular quilts is difficult..." consider that even if your quilt is a rectangle you'll only have to figure out the match two times at the most. "But there are four borders! Won't I have to figure out the match four times?" you say. No. One matching solution serves for the two side borders of the quilt, and another solution will work for both the top and bottom borders. You can deal with two matching points. It's when you have to figure out what to do on all four sides of the quilt that marking can get discouraging. When you're stuck matching all four borders, you have usually slapped down a quilting design in a corner and then proceeded to mark. Of course every side is a challenge! Remember that when marking a border, you will have to figure out matching two times at the most. If you're set on a square quilt, the matching only needs to be figured once.

Your job when marking a wavy line design, such as a cable, is to make any variations in the size of the waves invisible to the viewer. You don't want an admirer to be aware of where you connected the designs. The border should appear as a smooth and flowing design. The extra effort comes in making a paper model of your borders, one for the two sides and another for the top/bottom. Shelf paper is the quilt marker's secret weapon.

Preparing to Mark a Quilt

The following directions are for marking a quilt with a cable border design with corners, and for making the border and its corners flow together seamlessly.

When you use a stencil right off the shelf of the local quilt shop, you will need to put some registration lines on the stencil. These guiding lines ensure you'll be able to mark the design straight on the quilt. Use a permanent marker and mark the stencil in this manner:

◆ Measure the width of the stencil design (the cut-out motif only), divide that figure by two, and mark a line that shows the half-width of the design all through the design. This divides the cable in half visually and will be very helpful later in the marking process.

◆ On the stencil, mark off the corners of the cable as squares.

◆ Draw a 45-degree line at the corners of the stencil.

Preparing the Borders for Marking

Just as you marked the halfway line on the stencil, you need to mark the halfway line on the quilt border. Of course, you'll use a very different marker than you did on the stencil! Registration lines on the quilt should be marked with an easy-to-dust-away chalk. I suggest a rolling chalk wheel.

◆ Measure the width of the quilt border, discounting the 1/4" that eventually will be covered by the binding. Draw the halfway line around all four borders, using the wheel and a ruler to guarantee straight lines. At the middle of each border, draw a line that divides that border in half. These are called midpoints and are comparable to the north-south-east-west lines on a map.

◆ Mark off the corners as squares, and

◆ Mark a 45-degree line through the corner squares.

Now all the registration marks on the stencil and the border are complete.

The Purpose of Registration Lines

I'm sure most of you have already caught on to how the registration lines on the stencil and the border interact. The registration lines match. You won't make the mistake of running your design uphill or downhill if your stencil's halfway line lies directly on top of your border's halfway line. Quilt marking has just gotten a whole lot easier!

If the border design you want to mark is wide or complex there is one other intervening step that will make your border marking a breeze. It's rarely talked about in quilting classes since most quilting teachers take a hit-or-miss attitude toward quilt marking. Like everybody else, they're baffled about lengthening or shortening designs, and few people, except printers and graphic artists, use registration lines. If you have been marking registration lines and working out how to best use stencils, pat yourself on the back. Now you have a name for the process, and this text will assist you the next time one of your friends asks you to mark the borders for her quilt.

Making a Paper Model for Borders

Measure the height of your border and discount the extra 1/4" that will be covered by the binding. Measure the border length from the corner square to the other corner square. Do this for the sides and again for the top/bottom borders. (The corner squares do not figure in this calculation because you have already marked them.) Take two strips of paper (this is when a roll of shelf or drawing paper comes in handy), one of each length, and mark one "Sides" and the other "Top/Bottom." Now the fun begins. You'll use the stencil on the paper model first before marking the quilt. You can adjust the design, make notes to yourself, and not worry about soiling the quilt with messy or inaccurate marking. What seems like an extra step is actually a time and sanity saver.

The stencil has its registration lines already marked. The paper model is the length and width of one of the quilt's borders. This model includes the corners on either end. The model is marked with registration marks that echo the chalk registration marks put on the actual quilt border.

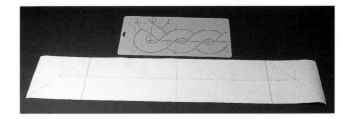

The stencil and the paper model.

In general, you'll discover that the ideal place for matching border designs is not at the corners and not at the exact middle of the border—it's somewhere to either side of the midpoint. That way the matching is not obvious to the viewer. In a cable, a design with waves that undulate over and under, you may also find that slightly adjusting the sizes of the waves will be an acceptable matching solution.

The Paper Solution

On the paper model, draw two corners in the squares you marked using the stencil's corner design. Do not flip the stencil over when you mark corners—simply move the stencil from one side to the other. The corners will look alike. Then quickly move the stencil along the paper model, keeping the halfway mark on the stencil on top of the halfway line on the paper. Before drawing the waves of the stencil, decide if the number of possible waves fits well within that border. In the case of the sample quilt in the photographs the last cable wave would have been quite a bit smaller than the other waves. It would have been obvious that the cable was squeezed into that border. But if the "eyes" of the cable (the flattened ovals at the center of the design) were all moved about 1/4" to the left, it would slightly reduce each cable wave in size, and the minute difference in the size of the cables on the width and length of the rectangular quilt would not be noticeable.

Using the stencil to figure the repeats of the cable on the paper model.

After the eyes of the cable are drawn with the stencil, go back and add the tops and bottoms of the waves using the stencil. Use the stencil as much as possible for consistency in the design.

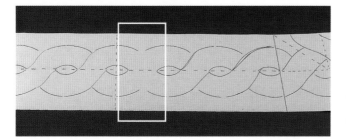

Where to make adjustments on the paper model border.

It's clear that the place for adjusting the cables is where they cross each other. That means there is a minimum of fine tuning—in terms of freehand drawing—that you must draw on the model and later mark on the quilt border. Use the stencil for reference when drawing the connecting over/under cable strands.

From Paper to Fabric

After you're satisfied with your paper model, pin it above the border on the quilt and repeat the steps in chalk on the fabric.

Mark the corners first, then the eyes of the cable.

After getting the corners marked, duplicate the model's cables on the border. Align a carpenter's square with the left side of a cable eye on the model. Follow the carpenter's square arm down to the halfway registration line on the quilt border and make a

dot there. After having marked all the left eye points, flip the carpenter's square over and repeat the marking, bringing down the right points of the eyes to the quilt border.

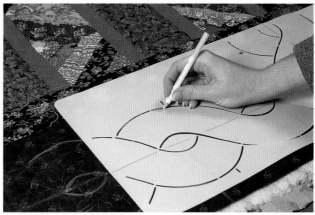

Continue marking the new, improved cable on your quilt.

Use as much of the stencil as possible when marking the cable on the quilt. Draw the tops and bottoms of the cables above and below the eyes and leave only the small areas where the cables cross to be filled in freehand.

Completing the new cable.

Draw the crossing cables in the open areas. Don't worry—it's only an inch or two of freehand marking!

Background quilting really makes the cable stand out.

Use a large rotary cutting square, set exactly on the diagonal, to mark background lines at a 45-degree angle. The right angle of the square will guarantee you can consistently mark these lines at the correct angle. The width of the spaces between background lines looks best when the lines are smaller in scale than the cable strands.

Border and background quilting.

The cable design was quilted in pale yellow thread so it would stand out, while the background lines were quilted in a darker shade of rose to make them less conspicuous.

Perfection Is Not Required

The more compulsive among you will likely be a bit taken aback at this casual approach to marking with a stencil. What you had hoped was that I'd let you in on the secret formula that makes all border quilting designs meet exactly. Sorry, the formula does not exist. We make different border widths and lengths, and no one I know consults the measurements of the border stencil before sewing that border on their quilt. The happy news is that no one will notice the slight dissimilarities in the length of the waves unless you hand them a ruler and say, "See, here's where it's off a bit."

What You've Just Learned

Perhaps you're asking, "Are all border designs this challenging to mark?" Let me assure you—a wide over-and-under cable is about the most formidable design to mark on a quilt border. Any other designs you are likely to think of will be easier than this one. If you are disheartened because marking a cable sounds difficult, reflect a moment.

Here are the helpful things you learned about quilt marking:

◆ Registration lines on the stencil and on the quilt border ensured your marking would be straight.

◆ You used inexpensive paper to figure out the matching solution before you started to mark the quilt and made a model to guide you when marking.

◆ The carpenter's square allowed you to be confident of duplicating on the quilt exactly what you had drawn on the paper model.

◆ When you used as much of the stencil as possible when marking, you cut down on the marking time.

Certainly not all borders require that you make a paper model or adjust the elements in a design. Only wide and complex designs and over/under designs, such as cables, demand this extra effort. Most of the time you can use one of the ten methods of getting around matching borders and corners. But sometimes you want to use a flowing design on your quilt's borders and show off your skill. An interwoven design will always get attention. The paper model method insures that you will mark that cable with ease and grace.

After marking fancy designs, any well-quilted quilt will also need background quilting. While background quilting is not as visually exciting as fancy motifs, it both ensures the quilt will last for years, and makes the fancy motifs stand out in contrast.

Bonnie Bus achieved a beautiful balance between piecing, color interplay, and quilting in this quilt she made as a marriage gift for her brother and his wife. Circular lines cross over the patchwork while sashiko designs in white and pink thread embellish the open white spaces.

There are debates about how far apart quilting lines can be stitched to keep the batting in place. Batting manufacturers offer their recommendations on their product's packaging. The trend right now is to assure customers they can get away with minimal quilting and that quilting with their product is "fast and easy." All the guidelines that companies state for their products ought to be taken with a grain of salt. Decide for yourself how far apart background lines should be marked on your quilt. Three factors will determine those proportions: what looks good to you, how much time you want to spend quilting the quilt, and how much quilting is required to keep the layers of top, batting, and backing together.

Background quilting is the plain step-child of quilt marking but it is more important in the construction of the quilt than the other motifs. Some references to

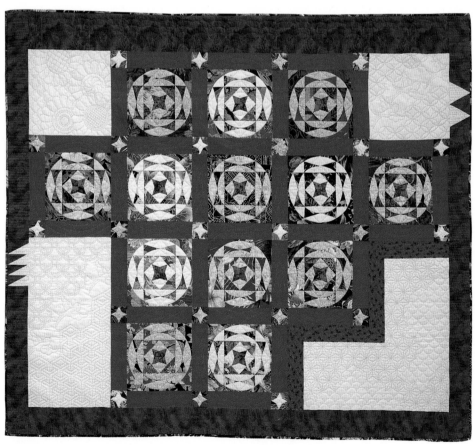

Wedding Quilt by Bonnie Bus. 73" x 82". Collection of Richard and Sherry Cummings.

background quilting are scattered throughout this text; see Chapter 6, Background Designs, page 32; and Chapter 3, In the Opinion of the Professionals, page 16.

Straight-Line Designs

Here are some strategies for marking straight-line background quilting.

◆ Determine the proportions of grid quilting from the block construction. A diagonal crosshatch design is drawn corner to corner across pieced blocks and meets the side of the blocks at the seam intersections.

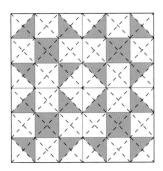

Diagonal crosshatch

A straight grid can follow the piecing seams or it can hit between the seams at even intervals. See Mary Mashuta's explanation of her two-step process of grid quilting on page 17. **Grid quilting marked this way is stronger than "in-the-ditch" quilting.**

A vertical/horizontal grid could follow the seams of the patchwork exactly (in-the-ditch quilting), but the quilting would almost be invisible. Instead, mark a straight grid by measuring between the seam lines at even intervals and superimpose that over the patchwork.

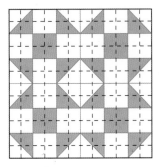

Straight grid

◆ If the quilt top has an antique feel, hanging Diamonds might be a suitable background. One set of lines, either horizontal or vertical, is marked first, and then a second set of lines is marked that crosses these at a 45-degree angle. Use a carpenter's square or an architect's triangle to assure a true 45-degree angle when drawing.

Other straight-line patterns include diagonal lines marked at a 45-degree angle. These groups of lines can be marked at even intervals or they can vary with some lines further apart.

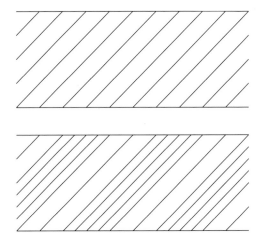

Diagonal lines can also be marked at different intervals to give more visual interest.

A number of Ohio Amish quilts display an interesting straight-line variation called Railroad Tracks. These are two lines marked about 1/2" apart followed by a space of about an inch, then another set of lines 1/2" apart and another space. When the Amish marked quilts in this manner, the seams of the patchwork did not dictate the placement of the lines. Railroad Tracks were often marked across pieced blocks, and also used as a background for fancy quilting designs. See the photo on page 19, "Amish Baskets."

Another quilting design indigenous to a particular region is the X-shaped straight-line quilting found on quilts from coastal North Carolina. My friend Rachel has a Log Cabin quilt made by her grandmother in the 1930s marked in this fashion. Rachel calls it the "Core Banks Cross."

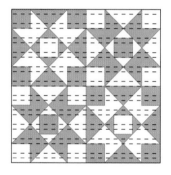

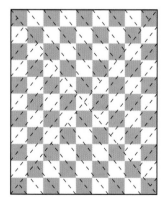

Two ladies stood at opposing corners of the quilt that was stretched full length on the frame and then snapped a chalked string across the surface of the quilt. Then they moved to the other corners and

snapped the chalk string again, thus marking the whole quilt in a large X. Finally, parallel lines were chalked in each quadrant of the X with a yardstick as a guide. The only caution about the Core Banks Cross is that when a quilt is quilted in this manner and then folded in quarters, it can develop a permanent crease in the center of the quilt. Folding the quilt in thirds will eliminate this problem.

Curves as Background Quilting Designs

Filling spaces in the background of appliqué blocks can be accomplished by echo quilting. While the first round of quilting might be marked, the quilter soon learns to estimate the spaces between the lines and rarely marks her echo quilting beyond the initial shape. See "Pieced Whig Rose" on page 48.

In the block below, echo quilting radiates out from the motif like ripples on a pond.

Another group of curved line designs has its origins in the classic clamshell pattern seen in both English and American quilts. The smallest clamshells were marked around the quilter's own thimble as she worked, but larger ones were marked with the aid of teacups and saucers. My theory is that the all-over waves common on so many Southern quilts are the country cousins of classic clamshells. Contemporary quilters are also showcasing curved line backgrounds in loops and swirls of machine quilting that add an almost Art Deco feeling to their modern quilts. This type of quilting adds visual movement to a quilt when the scale is not too small.

Still other background designs that have found favor with quilters are the sashiko designs of traditional Japanese garments and quilts. "Seven Treasures" is an old sashiko design, but it is also found in English and American quilts and called "wineglass" or "teacup" quilting after the homemade templates used to mark it.

One final caution about marking background quilting after quilting fancy motifs: **Make sure the proportions of the background design are smaller than the proportions of the fancy design.** For instance, if you've marked a cable design with strands about 1" thick, then mark a background design such as 45-degree lines 1/2" apart. This contrast will subtly lift the curves of the cable into the light since the more dense background lines will flatten the surface of the quilt.

Keep in mind the importance of contrast when choosing both your fancy and background designs. Consider that a technique such as graceful curved appliqué shows best against straight-line quilting as shown in Stars Over Carolina at right.

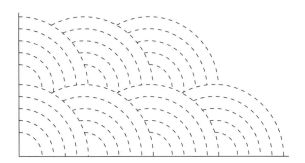

Tiny clamshells

Freeform quilting

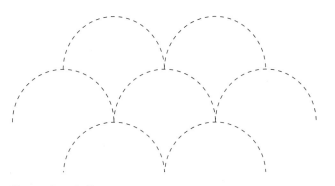

Classic clamshells

Seven Treasures

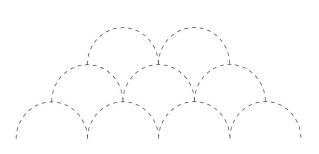

All-over waves or fans

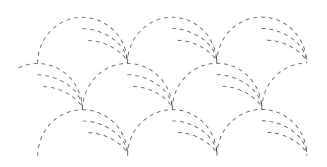

Pampas Grass is a graceful interpretation of grasses blowing in the wind.

Also allow for contrast within the quilting designs themselves—curves versus lines will always show both motifs to advantage.

In Stars Over Carolina the pieced block is Sarah's Star, a Quaker signature block, while the appliqué blocks are new designs. Double outlines surround the appliqués while their background is straight-line quilting that extends over into the pieced blocks.

Feather motifs in the outer triangles are complemented by straight lines of quilting. Whatever your preference in background quilting, think of that extra time as time spent bonding with your quilt. Remember those additional hours of quilting will add years to the life of your quilt. If you compete in quilt shows, rest assured extensive background quilting never fails to impress. See Chapter 13, Quilting from the Judges' Point of View.

Stars Over Carolina. 84" square. The 1997 raffle quilt for the Crystal Coast Quilters Guild. Designed by Kathy Cannon and Pepper Cory, top made by members of the guild, hand quilted by Judy Epps. From the collection of Gretchen Blaugher Gockley.

Nine-Patch Study. 45" x 55". A wall-hanging in a modern interpretation of the Nine-Patch pattern called "Puss in the Corner." All-over background quilting marked in concentric circles ignores the seams of the pieced blocks and helps unite the composition. Collection of the author.

Pieced Whig Rose. 76" square. Echo quilting outlines the pieced flowers of the blocks while zig-zag lines are quilted over the sashing. Made in Pitt County, North Carolina between 1875 and 1900. From the collection of Lynn and Will Gorges.

For a long time I searched for an easy method to make my own stencils. I wanted stencils that looked like the store-bought ones—stencils made of sturdy plastic, with slots wide enough to accommodate a chalk-marking pencil. All the directions I could find were for flimsy stencils cut with a double-blade craft knife. The blades did cut a double channel in the thin plastic, but tended to waver from the lines of the design. I still had to go back and trim the channels at the start and end of each cut. While I tried to do a good job, in the end I was too frustrated to adopt the method.

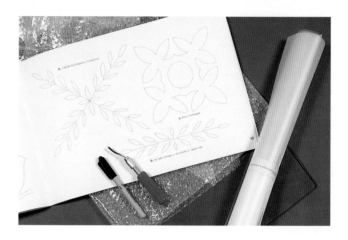

Directions also contradicted one another and no one could agree whether the stencils cut with the double-bladed knife should be cut over a craft mat or on a pane of glass. Finally I met an interesting man at a craft show in Indiana. His name was Samuel Graber and I saw him making a quilting stencil. Mr. Graber promised to show me how to cut quilting stencils if I visited his wife's quilt shop. I turned up bright and early the next morning and Sam took me under his wing and shared his method of making stencils. This technique of cutting quilting stencils has served me well for years. Thanks to Mr. Graber's generosity, you will now be able to make stencils as well.

Supplies for Making Stencils

Purchase a large, double-thick pane of glass as a cutting surface. Get a piece about the size of a placemat (12" x 15" inches) at the local glass shop and ask them to abrade (sand) the edges and corners so they are smooth and the corners rounded. When you're not using the glass surface, store it in a "pillow case" made from bubble-wrap packing material.

The cutting knife is an X-Acto #5 knife, stock number 3205. The blade that comes packaged with the knife is not the one you'll use to carve stencils. Instead you will use the X-Acto 3/32" U-Veiner gouge blade. The stock number is 156 and the blades come packaged two in a card. Both of these items are available at hardware, art supply, or craft stores. Sometimes this size blade may not be on the shelf but the store can order them for you. Buy a box (twelve packages) if you plan to do much carving. Both wood carvers and artists who make their own linoleum block cuts are familiar with this blade.

The plastic I prefer for making stencils is a polyethylene plastic called Mylar in a .15mm thickness. It is slightly opaque but you can see through it. The back is slightly textured, which makes for a non-slip stencil. Often you can find this plastic sold in quilt stores for templates but it is also available by mail. Other sorts of plastic, such as Styrene, do not lend themselves to this cutting method.

You will need a design to trace on the plastic to translate into stencil form. There are books of quilting designs, designs in magazines, and of course those of your own imagination. For your first designs, don't try anything overly large or complex. Pick something simple. With practice, your dexterity with the tools will develop and your wrist will get stronger. Also, I would never reproduce a design that was commercially available. Your time is worth a great deal more than the modest cost of, for instance, a feather wreath design. Make your own stencils when you want original designs or when you are tracing the design from a book.

How to Cut a Quilt Stencil

1. **Choose the Design.** Trace the design you want to cut as a stencil on a piece of plastic somewhat larger than the design. You can always cut down the plastic after making the design, and you need the extra plastic at the edges to hold as you cut. Do not attempt to cut a stencil with a piece of plastic barely bigger than the design: you will be asking for trouble. Too little plastic to hold on to makes the stencil difficult to cut and your chances of accidentally cutting yourself greatly increase. Better to be safe than sorry.

Tracing the Design.

2. **Planning the Bridges in the Stencil.** Look at the design. Where any two or more lines intersect you will need to leave a bridge (uncut area) about $1/4$" long. Bridges are necessary to hold the stencil together, and $1/4$" is so short a distance that anyone can freehand the connecting line. If you're new to stencil making, circle the line intersections so you stop cutting there and leave a bridge.

3. **The Right Blade for Cutting Stencils.** Remove the blade that came packaged with the X-Acto knife handle. The chuck (the crosshatched metal collar between the blade and handle) unscrews to loosen the eye of the chuck. Carefully pluck the blade out and discard it or give it to a woodworker who will use it. Insert the gouge blade and tighten the chuck. Make sure the blade has slid all the way into the chuck. Just before the chuck is really tight, push down a bit on the hip of the blade to seat it well in the chuck. The "scoop" of the blade will be up toward you when you use the knife. Be careful, as the gouge blade is sharp at its end.

4. **Beginning to Cut the Stencil.** Choose a point at intersecting lines to begin cutting. The knife handle should nest comfortably in the palm of your hand and your forefinger should point out over the hip (wide upper part) of the blade. Keep your hand and forearm, grasping the knife, almost perpendicular to the surface of the plastic as you push the blade of the knife into the plastic.

Starting to Cut the Stencil.

Lean the knife back *ever* so slightly toward you, pushing down and away from yourself as you follow the outline of the design. The blade will slide along the glass and start to carve up a little curl of plastic in the groove of the blade. Always push the knife *away* from you. After one or two inches of cutting, wiggle the blade a little and pop the plastic curl up and out of the cut channel.

The little vein of plastic created by the knife blade will curl over the tip of the blade. As you stop cutting, flip the blade up and the curl will pop out of the channel.

In your first attempts at stencil cutting, you'll likely gouge a lot of plastic, make some raggedy looking stencils, and as often scoop the blade out of the plastic just when you were trying to push it forward. Don't be discouraged. Everybody does it. You've probably never used these tools in this way before. **The real secret to stencil cutting is to have a sharp blade and to keep the angle of your wrist and forearm at a right angle rather than let your arm drop down parallel to the glass surface.**

Remember this: Wiggle the blade and push down, continue pushing down as you push the knife away from you, and cut along the design lines. Getting the feel for stencil cutting is a bit like learning to ride a bike. Once you've cut a channel with the blade, you'll understand that the angle is everything. Words are inadequate to accurately describe stencil cutting because it is a physical act. By practicing and developing hand-eye coordination you will begin to get it. Keep cutting.

Practice your cutting technique on a spare piece of plastic. Every time I cut a stencil I do a little practice cutting beforehand as a warm-up exercise.

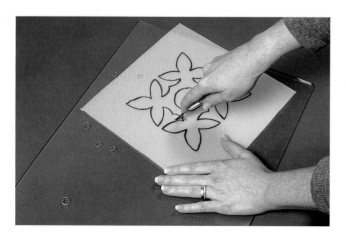

Continuing to Cut the Stencil.

5. **Continue to Cut the Stencil.** As you push the blade through the plastic, you'll discover that you only want to make channels about two inches long or less. Bridges not only keep the stencil together—they're also the "resting places" in the cutting.

As you cut around the outline of the design, move the plastic occasionally to ensure your hand is out of the way and the cutting knife can be held at a comfortable and safe angle. I cannot stress enough the importance of moving the plastic. Once when I was intent on cutting a curved design, I did not stop to move the plastic and inadvertently pushed the knife toward myself. I still have the long grooved scar along my left hand to warn students of the dire results of not handling stencil cutting tools properly.

Completed Stencil.

6. **All Finished and Ready to Use.** Clean up the little plastic curls that have accumulated and check your stencil to make sure you've carved all the lines. If you gouged the plastic outside the design lines, simply remedy the mistake with a tape patch. Remember that a stencil is only the means to convey a design on to the quilt, so it doesn't have to be a work of art. Some of my homemade stencils are rather ratty and look as if they've been rescued from the trash. Until now no one knew the elegant tulip branch I love to quilt on borders is marked with a ragged homemade stencil. The point is you are now able to make your original designs in stencil form, or finally get those beautiful designs out of magazines you've been admiring and transform them into

workable marking tools. All the quilting designs in the world are now possible.

If you plan to mark a block a particular size, you can now trim the Mylar square to that size.

Other Cutting Tools

A stencil burning tool called an electric knife is available. This electric knife has a wooden handle (to protect your hand from being burned) and a metal spike shaft that ends in a conical point. To burn plastic for quilting stencils, the manufacturer suggests you file down the metal point to a blunt tip. Like the gouge knife, this tool should only be used over a double-pane glass surface. The cutting process is slower than the gouge and the melted plastic tends to build up around the tip. You must stop and clean off the tip from time to time. Be careful—it's very hot! My main objections to the stencil burning pen are that it's not as fast as knife-carving a stencil, the process is messy, and the odor from the melting plastic compels you to use this tool only in a well-ventilated room.

Sharpening and Preserving Blades

The gouge blades from X-Acto are not meant to be permanent tools. They are only nominally sharpened, and sometimes must be cleaned when you remove them from the packaging because the blades are coated with oil to prevent rusting. Rust can still develop in humid climates, and if there's rust on a new blade brush it off with a little brass bristle brush. Check the blades and clean them before starting to cut. When the blade gets rough during the cutting process, stop and sharpen it. To sharpen the blade, stroke it backward about ten times on fine-gauge silicon carbide sandpaper.

Look at the end of the blade from time to time as you stroke it along the sandpaper. Make sure you're not angling it to one side but rather retaining the U formation of the original blade. Eventually the blade will wear out and you should discard it for a new one. I have also tried a straight-handled woodcarver's gouge to cut stencils but the results have been less than satisfactory. The "dog leg" design of the X-Acto craft knife handle is shorter and much easier to control against the plastic and the glass.

Why You Want to Learn to Cut Your Own Stencils

You're never going to save a pile of money by cutting your own quilt stencils. In fact, you may spend a bit as you acquire the tools. It's impossible to make a profit selling handmade stencils. I know—some friends of mine tried it and although they developed wrists as strong as those of professional wrestlers, they found they could not compete with the low prices of manufactured stencils. Here's why you want to know how to make your own quilting stencils—you'll never again feel at the mercy of a store's inadequate or uninspiring choice of stencils. You'll realize that your own ideas for designs can be made real. Learning to make stencils is a great confidence booster. But don't waste your time cutting a stencil in a familiar pattern that you can buy at the store. Your time is worth more than that, and besides, stencil designers still need their jobs.

Preserving a Design Found on an Old Quilt

When you see an interesting design on an old quilt, first research the quilt's origins. This is called the provenance. If you bought an antique quilt at a shop ask the shop owner where the quilt came from, how old she thinks it is, etc. If the quilt is in a museum, recording the design is quite a different proposition.

Tracing a Design from an Antique Quilt

First measure the area of the quilting design you want to record. Purchase a healthy chunk of clear flexible plastic, which comes on a roll, at a hardware or fabric store. This plastic is the clear vinyl used to cover picnic tables or to make temporary storm windows. Get the widest width you can in the lightest available weight. You may have to sew two or more lengths of the plastic together if you plan to trace a complete quilt. When sewing lengths of plastic together, secure the pieces temporarily with masking tape—don't use straight pins as they will pierce the plastic—thread your machine with strong thread, use an old needle, and sew with a longer-than-average stitch length.

The tool to use for marking on the plastic is a black permanent marker. Buy the pen with the medium-fine tip. To test markers for the job, take a scrap of the clear plastic with you to the art supply store. Stand in front of the markers and test them on the plastic. You want the one that makes the darkest line, dries the quickest, and doesn't smudge.

Lay the Plastic Over the Quilt— Be Careful!

Cover the design on the quilt with the plastic, making very sure ample plastic also covers the area around the design. Use caution, since you will transfer the design in permanent marker and you don't want to get any extra marks on the quilt. It is also a good idea to examine the clear plastic before you lay it on the quilt to see if there are any minute holes in the plastic. Once I missed a tiny hole in the plastic. As I traced, I inadvertently dotted marker onto a fine old quilt. I am still doing penance to the quilt's owner for that mistake.

Then put on the radio because what follows is not rocket science. You will trace the design as you see it through the plastic, stitch to stitch. This may sound tedious, but what you will discover is that as the quilting designs emerge, you will become very focused in your work.

Many quilting designs are familiar, so why can't you just draw the inside circle of that feather wreath and be done with it? Because, just about the time you confidently draw that circle, you will realize the design is an open shape, perhaps a lyre and not a wreath at all, and you'll need to start over.

Record the Design Accurately

Historical accuracy is important at this stage, even if you later decide to modify the design. If the feathers are lumpy and bumpy, draw them that way because that's how they were on the original quilt. After recording the design accurately, label it with the date, your name, and any information you have gathered about the quilt.

The odd-looking eagle below, probably drawn freehand, is the quilting motif on an 1850s Rising Sun quilt from Michigan. By placing plastic over the quilt, I could see through to trace the image onto the plastic.

Using the directions from Chapter 9, I transferred the new eagle design from the tracing paper to a square of Mylar and carved a stencil. The only tricky part was cutting the basket weave over/under from the head of the eagle down to the wavy stripe on its chest. Lots of bridges had to be left in the stencil in this area, and as I mark a quilt using this stencil, I'll fill in the connecting lines.

Record the Design Accurately.

Re-Draw the Design if Desired.

The "New" Eagle Design.

Storing Your Design

After recording your old quilting design, put tissue over the plastic and carefully roll it on a section of a cardboard tube (the ones carpet comes rolled on) and store it in a cool, dry place. Some brands of vinyl come with their own tissue covering since the plastic tends to build up static electricity as it slides across itself. The tissue serves two purposes. It both prevents the plastic from sticking to itself and stops the designs from "lifting" onto other surfaces. Keep the plastic designs away from heat (no attic storage) and light (when not using the designs roll them up) since eventually the markings do tend to fade. This takes years but it will eventually happen.

What You Don't Do to Trace a Design

I have occasionally seen people at a quilt show hold tracing paper up to a quilt and attempt to trace the design. This is a poor substitute for tracing directly from the piece and the tracing paper can rip, resulting in pencil marks on the quilt. Don't do it. And as a matter of quilt show etiquette, always ask permission if you want to take photographs. If you see a quilt with designs you want to record, ask the owner's permission, make an appointment to go see her and the quilt later (when it's not hanging), take your plastic and marker, and do the job right. Offer to do an extra tracing for her as a favor for allowing you to copy her pattern.

Working with a Museum

If you've seen an interesting design on an antique quilt in a museum, there are steps you can take to establish trust with the institution so you can gain access to the quilt. Start with a complimentary letter to the head curator of the artifacts at that museum. Tell them you've seen the quilt, loved it, and would like to examine it more closely. Show enthusiasm and respect. Ask to make an appointment to see the quilt and record the quilting design. Follow up on this letter two weeks later.

Folks in museums are often overworked and behind in their correspondence, so the ball is in your court for developing this relationship. What you want to do is to get to know staff members, such as the curator of textiles, at the museum. Emphasize that you can record the design without needing to physically touch the quilt. Bring in some plastic, a marker, and one of your own quilts to demonstrate how you transfer the design. It's a good idea also to bring in your own white gloves to show them you know how to handle antique textiles.

Basically, what I've learned about museum curators is this simple truth: in their heart of hearts, they guard that collection as if it belongs to them. That's what makes them good caretakers. In all your dealings with museums, recognize the staff's protective instincts about the artifacts. Offer to transfer other designs, or volunteer some time at a museum event. It's only good politics to give something to the institution when they have let you trace designs from their quilts.

Research in the Museum Setting. If you are looking for quilting designs on old quilts in a museum's collection, try looking at the whole-cloth quilts first. Since the museum might have some but not call them by that name, search under the following headings: Quilts, All Quilted Quilts, Whole Cloth, White-on-White, Coverlet, Coverlid, Marseilles Spread, Bedspread, Marcell Spread, Furniture Padding, and Mattress Pad. When a white whole-cloth quilt became worn or tattered, it was sometimes dyed another color or was relegated to other uses. It might have been used as furniture padding or placed between the mattress and box springs of a squeaky bed. Many museums, especially small regional ones, are not up-to-date in their textile research and archiving. By working with a museum, you, as an informed quilter, can actually help the museum recognize and better care for their quilts.

Tracing the Design in the Museum. The steps for tracing from a museum quilt are the same for any other quilt, but you need to be especially careful when handling the museum's quilt. It will be brought out to you wrapped in a muslin covering and unrolled on tables covered with acid-free paper. Wear white gloves (the museum might provide these) as you examine the quilt. Be especially careful at the edges of the quilt as old quilts often fray at the binding.

As you trace designs from an old quilt in a museum collection, don't be surprised if everybody on the staff just "happens" to wander through the room where you're working. Most of them have never seen quilting stitches recorded, and consequently they have never really looked at quilting designs. As you trace the designs and they come to life in black lines on your plastic overlay, you will be gratified to hear comments like, "I never knew our quilts had designs like that on them! Wow, that's a lot of work! Did they do that all by hand?" You will help open their eyes and they will gain respect for the quilts in their collection.

Surprises in Old Quilts. Every once in a while, as you trace designs from an old quilt, you will realize the lines are resolving into some image you did not see when casually looking at the quilt. I have found dates and names quilted into old quilts. To get a preview of what the quilting designs might be, hold the back of the quilt up to a mirror. Many times the distance that mirror image provides will reveal nuances in the quilting you had not noticed before. One of the perks of quilt research is that you might discover something truly wonderful, hidden for years in the stitching, as you trace quilting designs from old quilts. See the Welsh quilt on page 8 for an example of a quilted date.

At a later date, you may want to make a stencil from a tracing you made from an old quilt. If you do and you enter the quilt quilted with that design in a show, give the quilting design information along with the other information you supply with the entry form.

Russian Sunflower Quilt. 76" x 84". A classic navy and white quilt made by Catharine McCormick of Indianapolis, Indiana in 1848. The winding vines quilted between the pieced blocks are complemented by little hearts tucked here and there in the foliage. This creative approach to marking reveals an experienced quilt designer at work. From the collection of Xenia Cord.

The designs on these pages come from several sources. A few were taken from my earlier books on quilting designs. Others were inspired by English quilting traditions. Some are based on the designs of quilt kits of the 1930s, and still others are my own creations.

Each design has an explanation of its origin, its size if reproduced exactly as seen on the page, and directions for use. You can enlarge these designs on a photocopying machine. You have my permission to do so when you are making a stencil for your own use. The usual copyright laws apply, however, so the designs can not be reproduced for resale.

Amish Cut-out. A simple design inspired by traditional Amish quilting designs. Measures 6" square. If you are new to cutting your own stencils, try this one as your first stencil.

Chain Design. An interlocking chain block that measures 4" square. This might be design #2 for you to try. Circle the over/under points of this design because you want to be careful to leave bridges there.

Angel Wing Corner. It fits snugly in the corners of a 3" border.

When marking within scallops, leave 1/2" between the design and the edge of the quilt.

Scallop Plume. A pretty plume that finishes a scalloped quilt edge beautifully, or it can be repeated in a border. Inspired by quilting on a kit quilt from the 1930s. The plume from tip to largest feather is 8" long, and the depth of the curve (measured as a half-circle) is 4". When marking as a repeat in a border, use the two largest feathers mirror-imaged for the corner design.

Welsh Heart. A traditional Welsh heart with spirals. Measures 6" wide across the top of the heart and is 5" in length. Fun to quilt!

Comforter Design.

Comforter Design. One-quarter of a rectangular design reminiscent of satin machine-quilted comforters of the 30s. When repeated four times, the design measures 12" x 18".

Heart and Hands. One-half of a block design suitable
for a friendship or wedding quilt. When mirror-imaged
(as seen above) the heart measures 10 $^1/_2$" high.

Baby Vine. A tiny vine border 1 $^1/2$" wide. Although this design ends with a leaf, if your border is longer, mark the vine continuously (after you've done the corners) and then come back and mark the leaves.

Compass Circle. Playing with a compass can result in some interesting designs. This one measures 5 $^1/2$" across.

British Plait. When measured as an "X" it is 6" square, but marked in a cross it measures 8 ^{1}/$_2$".

Doves. Two kissing doves and a heart are a continuous line 2" design.

Elizabeth's Star. Don't faint! This design looks incredibly complex because it has been reduced to the size of this page. Take this to a photocopy machine that will make 11" x 17" copies. Enlarge this design until it measures 8" from the center of the hearts to the star points. Make two copies and combine for an elegant 16" star in the classic style of Elizabeth Sanderson.

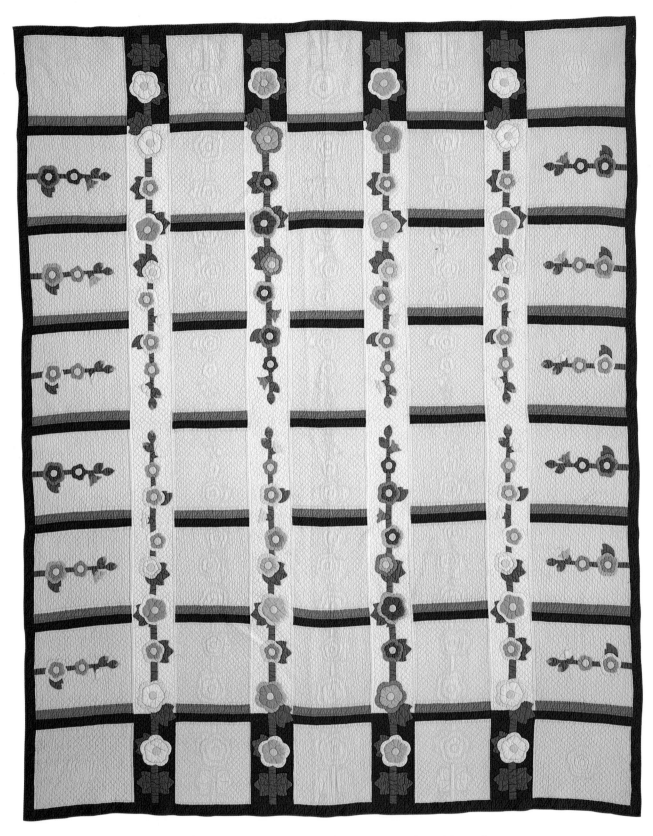

Hollyhocks. 77" x 92". Made in the 1930s after a design by a Mrs. Frank H. Trapp from Taylorville, Illinois, this cheerful medley of solid-color flowers in a vertical appliqué format became Mountain Mist Pattern #49. The quilting marked in the yellow rectangles echoes hollyhock blossoms while the background is grid quilted in $1/2$" crosshatching. From the Mountain Mist Historical Quilt Collection/The Stearns Technical Textiles Company.

Caring for Quilt Stencils

All commercial quilt stencils have holes for hanging, either round or butterfly holes; take the manufacturer's hint and hang your stencils to store them. Don't jam them in a drawer or file. Stencils are likely to get bent, catch on each other, or get torn if they are laid flat. Sorting your stencils by design type makes retrieving them easy. Buy some inexpensive shower curtain hooks and sort the stencils by type. Hang the large border designs together, the small borders together, and the block designs together. Hang your stencils somewhere in sight of where you usually sew and quilt. There is a real and practical reason for hanging the stencils within sight of where you work.

Stencils in Sight=Quilting in Mind

Since most of us make our quilt tops and then decide what to mark on them, having those quilting designs omnipresent helps us stay conscious of the marking task ahead. It's similar to an artist having all his colors of paint out in front of him as he works. Having all your tools—stencils included—in sight keeps you aware of the overall process.

Blue Ribbons by Pepper Cory, quilted by Gail Hill. 47" square.

It's better to use traditional designs, ones you can be sure are common knowledge, than to use a design you later find is someone's original creation. Or, better yet, make up your own quilting patterns! Of course, commercially available stencils are exceptions. The manufacturers know you're going to use them, and will be pleased if your quilt is a prizewinner. But to be on the safe side, when I am making a competition quilt I put any pertinent information about the materials (fabrics, pattern, stencil) on the label on the back of the quilt. Then no one could ever say I claimed his or her work as my own.

Designs on Paper and Plastic

As you accumulate quilting designs on rolls of plastic, these rolls should be stored upright, with paper wrapped around them and lightly secured with a rubber band. I use a large wicker laundry basket to keep my pattern rolls neat. That same basket also serves for oversize rulers and empty mailing tubes. File your small designs recorded on paper until you want to make a stencil from them.

Mourning Dove. 47" square. Dorothy P. Porter was careful to credit Elly Sienkiewicz' book *Papercuts and Plenty* for inspiration for her wall-hanging, and worked with hand-dyed fabrics to create this subtle yet stunning wall hanging. Crosshatching marked one inch apart makes the delicate appliqué shapes "float" on the quilt's surface. Collection of the maker.

A few sources, such as Mormon Handicrafts (see Resources, page 77), sell whole-cloth quilt designs printed on large sheets of paper. These come folded but can be smoothed with a warm iron to flatten them, and then rolled around a tube for storage.

Whenever you are recording a quilting design, take down as much information as possible about the design. If you are tracing a design from a magazine or a book, note the title and issue number. Of course those designs from museum quilts (mentioned in Chapter 10) should each have the card catalogue numbers of the quilt written on a corner of the plastic tracing.

A word of caution: If you're making quilts for yourself and for your family and friends' pleasure, using designs from magazines and books is fine. But if you're making a quilt for a competition, particularly one in which you might win a cash prize, or if you are selling the quilt, think twice. Some quilting designs are copyrighted.

Cleaning Stencils

After a lot of marking, your stencils can become dirty with pencil and chalk marks. Clean your stencils in the tub with a couple of drops of dishwashing soap in warm water. Most marks will come right out with gentle rubbing with a wash cloth. Do not clean stencils too vigorously since you do not want to tear the bridges between the slots of the stencil.

If you have used a permanent pen to mark registration lines on a stencil, cleaning might have to be done a different way. Two chemicals are used to remove permanent marker lines from plastic stencils. One is acetone, found in nail polish remover, and the other is mineral spirits. When I use mineral spirits, I prefer the much less offensive-smelling turpenoid (synthetic turpentine) to old-fashioned turpentine. Place several sheets of newspaper over the table surface before cleaning stencils with chemicals. Then make another pad of paper toweling, three or four towels deep, on top of the newspaper. Lay the dirty stencil on this. Pour some acetone or turpenoid on a clean rag or wad of paper towels and

lightly rub the surface of the stencil. Pay special attention to where the marks might have gotten into the slots of the stencil. Rub until all the marks are gone. Turn the stencils over and also clean the back. The paper towel pad underneath the stencil will be saturated with the marker ink. At this point, I usually cart the stencil off to the tub to be further cleaned.

Such care may seem like a lot of fuss, but consider that unless you damage a stencil, it lasts a lifetime. I have stencils twenty years old that I use regularly. After cleaning, dry the stencils between two towels and re-hang them on their hooks.

Mending Stencils

If you should inadvertently tear a stencil, mend the tear with tape. If you jam a stencil in a drawer and bend it, hold the stencil in one hand and gently heat it with warm air from a blow dryer. When the stencil is quite warm along the crease, lay it flat under heavy books and let it cool to room temperature overnight. Sometimes a stencil is too badly damaged to revive. In that case, note its name and inventory number and order another from the quilt shop. When stencils were made of cardboard, quilters often bought more than one of their favorite design because they knew they'd "use up" the stencil in time. We're lucky that so many stencils in durable plastic are available to us. Remember, when you quilt with friends or go to workshops, label your stencils with your name.

When you make a quilt that will be judged in a competition or quilt show, looking at your quilting from the judges' point of view can be very illuminating. At a quilt show it's not uncommon for the judges to look at a hundred or more quilts in a day. They judge by categories (bed-size pieced quilts, bed-size appliqué quilts, wall hangings, garments, etc.) and then award ribbons within those categories. After all categories are judged, the judges award overall prizes such as Special Award for Artistic Merit, Judges' Choice, and Best of Show.

I judge quilt shows myself and find that the majority of judges I meet share my opinions. These are the standards that are applied to quilting:

1. There should be **enough** quilting in the quilt to hold it together well.

2. The designs should be suitable to the quilt type and should **enhance** the quilt top.

3. The quilting should be **evenly distributed** over the whole quilt top surface. There should not be any hills or valleys of batting or large flat unquilted areas, and especially no rippling along the edges of the quilt.

4. The quilt marking should be **erased**, so only the stitches are visible.

5. The workmanship, which includes the size of stitches, the regularity (evenness) of the stitches, and the stops and starts of stitching, should be **excellent**.

Perhaps you assume hand and machine quilting are always judged against each other and so one technique will be favored above the other by the judges. Not so. Depending on how the standards for that particular competition are written, machine and hand-quilted quilts may be grouped together or they may be separated. National and international shows are grouping machine and hand work together on the supposition that quilting is quilting and how it is accomplished is not the point, as long as it is done well. Regional or guild shows still tend to separate hand and machine work.

Exceptions to this view are the special prizes awarded by companies that have a particular stake in promoting one technique over another. For instance, a sewing machine company awards a special prize for machine quilting, or a thread company promotes hand quilting with a prize. I believe grouping machine and hand quilting together promotes a higher standard of workmanship. Machine quilters will realize their stitching will have to meet the traditional strict standards of hand quilting, while hand quilters are now on notice they need to quilt their quilts as thoroughly as machine quilters do in order to compete.

Enough Quilting

What is "enough" quilting in the judges' eyes? Most judges want to see a quilt that is very well quilted, and most admit to a preference for the flat, as opposed to the puffy, kinds of batting. They have seen enough quilts to know that minimal quilting will not last and that large unquilted areas mean trouble down the line as that quilt sees use. An unquilted area, when contrasted with pieced or appliquéd blocks and the color and seam lines of most quilts, looks like a still pond in the middle of a busy landscape. Of course there are some exceptions.

No More Monkeys Jumpin' on the Bed. 56" square. Contemporary quilt artist Alexandra Capadalis Dupré captured the happy feeling of children at play when she titled this multi-prizewinning quilt. Quilting here enhances the monkey appliqués while it adds diagonal lines across the light-colored plaids. From the collection of the maker.

An art quilt, such as a wallhanging, will never receive the physical wear of a bed quilt. However, while an art quilt may not require the same amount of structural quilting as a bed quilt, its quilting must still be of a high standard since it is viewed as art and the quilting needs to work artistically within the composition. A special liability of the art quilt is that because it is hung vertically, like a painting, the batting will "head south" if there's not enough quilting. Most judges concur that people need to quilt their quilts more, not less, no matter what the batting manufacturers say about their products.

Judges also admire background quilting, tedious though it might be to the quiltmaker, because such work really highlights fancy designs and showcases stitching ability. A deviation from this counsel is the omnipresent stippling many machine quilters apply to their quilts. Frankly, judges are growing tired of unimaginative stippling on everything. I've heard it called "no-brainer quilting," "scrambled eggs," and even "scribbling." Stippling is fun and it's fast—judges empathize with the attraction—but it cannot stand up in competition to well-thought-out original designs. Your stippled quilt may not get superior marks for creativity when judged. This is not to say that stippling is not welcome in the judging arena, but rather to forewarn you that all quilting, stippling included, is held to high standards both in technique and execution. My advice is to refer to a prize-winning quilt that used stippling to complement other quilting designs. Stippling, when used well, should fill in a limited space and not take over the quilt. An artistic decision to use all-over stippling, perhaps executed in exciting colored threads or metallics, should enhance the beauty of the quilt and not be an obvious shortcut to completion.

When a lot of nice quilting is evident on the topside of the quilt, judges love to turn the quilt over to see the effect of all those stitches on the back. If you're a good hand quilter, do not disguise your stitches with a busy print backing. Rather, stand up and take a bow by choosing a solid or subtle backing that shows your stitches. The judges' estimation of you goes up a notch or two when they see a beautifully quilted backing on your quilt. Machine quilters, on the other hand, often find that a subtle print back, in a color that relates to the theme of the quilt top, is "friendlier" to their style of stitching.

Evenly Distributed Quilting

Insufficient quilting is beginning to be a real bugaboo of quilt judges. They want to see quilting over the whole surface of the quilt. Please realize that very tight quilting in one area next to minimal quilting in the adjacent area of the quilt will make the batting eventually shift within the quilt. When a quilt is unevenly quilted, the batting puffs up in unquilted areas while it flattens down in heavily quilted areas. This contrast in tension within the body of the quilt takes its toll on the edges of the quilt. This problem was so prevalent at a recent show that the judges asked the scribe detailing our comments on a laptop computer to make an insertable comment with the following admonition: "Edges should be flat and straight with no rippling and corners should be square." The culprit was unevenly distributed quilting 90 percent of the time. Also note that heavy quilting in the middle of the quilt, contrasted with very little quilting in the borders of the quilt, is not artistically balanced and betrays that the quiltmaker was rushed for time. It's obvious that her intentions might have been good but she could not carry through her quilting plan.

Erasing Quilting Marks

Judges want quilting to look as though it was stitched freehand. Like magic, you should never be able to see how it's done. The stitches should speak for themselves. Judges realize many quilting designs are marked, but they do not like being distracted from the beauty of the quilt by lines still visible on the quilt top.

Morning Glory. 77" x 92". Made from the #35 Mountain Mist pattern dating to 1933, this modern version of Morning Glory follows the original quilting directions beautifully. Excellent workmanship plus outstanding color choice earned this quilt Second Place in the 1985 Mountain Mist National Quilt Contest. By Martha Skelton of Vicksburg, MS. Reprinted with permission from the Mountain Mist Historical Quilt Collection/The Stearns Technical Textiles Company.

Excellent Workmanship

Judges take several standards of workmanship into consideration. Quilting stitches should be even and small, and the evenness of the stitches is more important, generally, than their size. We are so conscious about trying for tiny stitches that we may think judges consider the size criterion the most important as they look at quilting. This is not the case. Judges give allowance for artistic choice and know that sometimes specialty threads do not show to full effect if stitched too small. Contrary to popular opinion, I have never seen a judge take out a ruler and measure stitches to the inch! A quilting stitch style called Big Stitch, first popular in the 1930s and recently revived, features stitches of about 1/4", executed in pearle cotton. Likewise, Sashiko—Japanese

Tumbling Blocks Frame Quilt. 79" x 90". This superb 1930s quilt features unique quilting designs in the white areas. The center is a medallion, the second lacy swags, and the third deco tree-like forms. From the collection of Barbara Woodford.

folk quilting—is judged primarily on the evenness of the stitches and not on size.

Starts and stops in stitching will be noticed if they are not done well. A start in hand quilting is noticeable when the first two to three stitches are larger and then even out. A stop is noticeable when a stitch is very tiny and almost disappears. Another stop clue is if the quilter has backstitched two to three stitches and those stitches are noticeably fatter. But the real tip-off is the little thread tail that peeps up in the immediate vicinity of the tiny stitch. The thread tail may be seen on either the top or the back of the quilt. Thread tails are verboten to judges; check your quilt for any before it's entered in competition.

Another stop/start problem occurs with sloppy machine quilting.

Some texts and teachers tell students to "dial down" (decrease) the size of their stitches when they want to end a line of stitching. Good machine quilters plan ahead and end their line of quilting in an inobvious seam. Likewise starts in machine quilting should begin inconspicuously. Another, more time-consuming approach to stops and starts in machine quilting is to leave fairly long tails of thread at the beginning and end of stitching. Your last step in the quilting process should be to thread a needle with the tails and then bury them in the batting as you would when hand quilting. Lest machine quilters reading this shake their heads in disbelief, the re-threading of the thread tails by hand is a competition trick and is certainly not necessary on all quilts.

Distinctions in Machine Quilting in Competitions

Just recently, some shows separated machine quilting into the following categories: machine quilting by the quiltmaker using her own sewing machine, machine quilting sent to a professional machine quilter who uses hand-guided machinery, and machine quilting by a professional using a preprogrammed design to quilt. The best policy is to be scrupulously honest when entering your quilt in any competition and ask for clarification if your quilt does not seem to fit the categories. Who knows? Perhaps they'll create a category especially for you!

Last Thoughts on Quilt Judging

While all competitions have their own specialized forms for judging, remember that quilting is considered under both Workmanship and Design. For most traditional quilts, Workmanship and Design are each about 50 percent of the quilt's score. But when considering art quilts, judges may lean more heavily on the design side of the scale, as those pieces must function as if they were paintings. Here the equation may be 40 percent Workmanship and 60 percent Design.

The purpose of writing all these details about judging quilting is not to discourage you from entering competitions. Quilt shows and exhibitions can be great fun and you'll benefit from the judges' comments when they say what they liked and disliked about your quilt. It's a great learning experience. Rather I hope you'll reread this chapter as you work on a quilt bound for competition and check that its quilting fulfills the "Five E's." Ask yourself:

- Is there **enough** quilting?

- Does the quilting **enhance** the quilt top?

- Is the quilting **evenly** distributed, with no unquilted areas and no side rippling?

- Are all the quilting marks **erased**?

- Is the workmanship **excellent**?

If you can answer yes to the above questions, you've done a masterful job of quilt marking and the resulting quilting is sure to impress the judges. Good luck and blue ribbons to you all!

Last Thoughts

When people have trouble marking their quilts, the difficulty usually centers on one of three problems:

- The quilter hasn't "changed gears" from the process of making her top, and has charged into marking the quilt top before thinking through the process.

- A paper model wasn't made first to work out changes and adjustments in designs.

- The wrong marking tools were used and the markings won't wash out.

Steps already suggested in the preceding text can remedy these problems. Chapter 5 addresses choosing quilting designs. Chapter 7 illustrates how to match designs and make adjustments to patterns. Chapter 4 details all the tools of the trade.

While I hope all the information in this book has been helpful, the most important bit of wisdom I want to impart is that marking is an integral step in making a fine quilt. Whether quilted by hand or machine or marked with the aid of stencils or tear-away patterns, marking is both challenging and creative.

What often constitutes the difference between a nice quilt and a fine quilt is the quilting. I base my judgement only partially on the execution of the stitches. Mostly I consider how it was quilted—what designs were marked and how they enhance the overall effect of the piece. Marking is technically the bridge between the flat two-dimensional quilt top and its gratifying final transformation. The quilting stitches, those little tiresome details we fret so much over, only follow the dictates of the marking. Marking makes a huge artistic difference to the quality and beauty of the quilt.

The process of marking does have a completely different rhythm than all the proceeding sewing. Have you ever played marching music? What happens in quilt marking reminds me of the Trio section of a march. First there's the strong melody that sets the mood for the march. Then follows the Trio, which is almost a time-out from the stirring strain since it is a softer and different tune altogether. Finally there's a return to the main melody and the march ends triumphantly. Think of constructing the quilt top as the main melody of your quilt. Then the marking is the Trio, the detour into a different tune. Of course your quilting draws all the elements together and you finally finish your quilt, triumphantly I hope, just like the march.

When I finish a quilt, it's often in the wee hours of the morning. There's no cheering audience to applaud my achievement, only the gentle sounds of distant snoring and an occasional sleepy cat that wanders out to inspect the latest project. But I've learned how to congratulate myself. I own several tapes of the music of John Philip Sousa, the greatest composer of march music. I hang the quilt on the wall, put on my earphones, and revel in the afterglow of my accomplishment as I hum along with the inspirational music. I wish for you the same satisfaction and joy in your quilting.

Samuel Bonnington Small, a hefty ginger cat, approves of the efforts of his quiltmaker-owner. Photo courtesy of Barbara Chainey.

Commonly Asked Questions About Quilt Marking

◆ **"I marked this quilt top a year ago in heavy black pencil. It's been stored in the attic and now that I'm ready to quilt it, I wonder, will the marks come out?"**

Time and heat are the enemies here. If you can locate the marking pencil you used mark a piece of fabric left over from piecing the top. Experiment on getting out the marks. First try fabric erasers, then graduate to cold water, warm water plus soap etc. A final artistic resort (making lemonade out of lemons) is to quilt your quilt using dark colored thread to visually minimize the contrast between the marking and the fabric. The quality of your stitching will be on show but you may find you like the bold effect of the prominent quilting.

Ensure (a Mountain Mist product) and Orvus Quilt Wash are two soaps you can try to eliminate pencil marks. They can be found in quilt shops or mail order (see Resources). A homemade solution can be made by mixing three parts rubbing alcohol, a couple of drops of white dish detergent, and one part water. Using a soft toothbrush dipped in the solution, gently brush the stitches, placing a towel under the quilt to absorb excess water. Blot dry with a clean cloth. For an allover bath, fill a bathtub 3/4 full with cold water and add 1/2 cup Woolite, 1/2 lb. salt, and 2 cups dry, nonchlorinated bleach. Dissolve and mix well before immersing the quilt. See **www.americana-roads.com/antiques.html** for complete directions for handling a large quilt.

On heavy chalk markings on dark fabric, white vinegar on a piece of dark soft cotton flannel can be rubbed over the marks. Do not saturate the material. Wait till it dries and then wash the whole quilt, if necessary, in cool water.

◆ **"I can't see any marker except the blue water marker on this busy fabric. Will it hurt to leave the markings on the quilt top for as long as it takes me to complete the quilting?"**

Water markers are wonderful tools but they should be used with all the cautions discussed on page 21. Above all, keep water-marked quilts away from heat that might set the marks, do not repeatedly re-mark designs once the quilt is basted (the marker tends to soak into the batting) and plan to wash that quilt as soon as you've finished it.

◆ **"I mark my quilts with really fine pencil lines but sometimes the marks are still visible after quilting. What can I do to avoid having to wash the whole quilt?"**

If your markings were done with a pencil, you can erase them as you go. Plan five minutes erasing time after you've stopped quilting for the day. If you quilt on a traditional frame, take a hard surface book and hold it underneath the frame, supporting the area you've just quilted. Very lightly erase the marks underneath the new stitches using a fabric eraser. If you quilt in a hoop, take your quilt out of the hoop and lay the area you've just quilted flat on a table. Again, lightly erase the marks.

Not having to wash your quilt also requires that you protect it while it's in progress. Cover the frame with a sheet. If there's tell-tale fur or a gentle sag in the frame when you return, Fluffy's been taking a siesta in your quilt "hammock." You might have to readjust the tension on the frame slightly before commencing work and somehow shut the cat out of the sewing room in the future!

If you quilt in a hoop, don't leave the quilt in the hoop for any length of time, not even overnight. Use a protective sheet to fold up around the quilt and remember to refold it different ways to minimize any creases.

◆ **"I took my quilt to a professional machine quilter. Since I didn't know how to mark the quilt, I told her to decide the quilting pattern. I got the quilt back and I don't like the effect. What should I have done?"**

A professional machine quilter uses her best judgement on what to quilt on your quilt but she is not a mind reader. Make sure you're dealing with a proficient machine quilter by asking to see samples of her work and inquire how long she's been in business. Show her some pictures of quilts with quilting you admire so she can get an idea of your taste in quilting and warn her if there's something you definitely don't want on your quilt. Buy good quality batting and backing as per her instructions. Expect to wait a bit longer for excellent work and pay a little more-just because she's using a machine doesn't mean she can quilt your quilt overnight.

◆ **"Do I always have to mark the whole quilt top before I start to quilt?"**

Many quilts can be marked one block at a time as you come to them in the quilting process. Think through your marking strategy: what designs to use, which markers work best, and what sort of background marking will compliment your quilt before you start to quilt. Refer to Chapter Four-In the Opinion of the Professionals-to get hints on the all- important step of planning your marking. See Chapter Eight-Matching Borders and Corners-to successfully mark borders.

If you do completely mark the quilt top before quilting, expect a few of the marks to rub out during quilting. But even if you must occasionally re-mark an area, that's much preferable to using some marker which might not wash out. A residue of chalk or pencil will assist you in repositioning your marks.

The only quilts that should be completely marked before commencing quilting are whole cloth quilts.

References

Allan, Rosemary. *North Country Quilts & Coverlets from the Beamish Museum County Durham.* Hindson & Company, Newcastle upon Tyne, England, 1987.

Berenson, Kathryn. *Quilts of Provence.* New York: Henry Holt and Company, 1996.

Bush, Karen. *Quilt as Desired!* Richmond, MO: Birdsong Collections, 1998.

Chainey, Barbara. *The Essential Quilter.* New York: Sterling, 1993.

———. *Quilt It!* Seattle, WA: That Patchwork Place, 1999.

Cory, Pepper. *65 Drunkard's Path Quilt Designs.* Mineola, NY: Dover, 1998.

———. *Multiblock Quilt Designs.* Mineola, NY: Dover, 1998.

———. *Quilting Designs from the Amish.* Lafayette, CA: C&T Publishing, 1985.

———. *Quilting Designs from Antique Quilts.* Lafayette, CA: C&T Publishing, 1987.

Cory, Pepper and McKelvey, Susan. *The Signature Quilt.* Saddle Brook, NJ: Quilt House Publishing, 1995.

Emms, Amy. *Amy Emms' Story of Durham Quilting.* Tunbridge Wells, Kent, England: Search Press Limited, 1990.

Fons, Marianne. *Fine Feathers.* Lafayette, CA: C&T Publishing, 1988.

Frost, Helen Young and Pam Knight Stevenson. *Grand Endeavors.* Flagstaff, AZ: Northland Publishing, 1992.

Kergreis, Solange. *Le Boutis.* Paris: Editions Didier Carpentier, 1993.

Marchbank, Brenda. *Durham Quilting.* London: Dryad Press Ltd, 1988.

McElroy, Roxanne. *The Perfect Stitch.* Chicago: Quilt Digest Press, 1998.

Miller, Phyllis D. *Encyclopedia of Designs for Quilting.* Paducah, KY: American Quilter's Society, 1996.

Osler, Dorothy. *Quilting.* London: Merehurst Limited, 1992.

———. *Traditional British Quilts.* London: B.T. Batsford LTD, 1987.

Walker, Michele. *The Passionate Quilter.* North Pomphret, VT: Trafalger Square Publishing, 1991.

Resources

Antique Quilts
Historic American Quilts
Barbara Woodford, Prop.
4775 S. River Rd.
Hanover, IL 61041
(815) 777-2009
http://www.historic-american.
com/woodford

Labors of Love
Jane Lury, Prop.
PO Box 352
Hillsdale, NY 12529
(518) 325-6486

Legacy Quilts
Xenia Cord, Prop.
Kokomo, IN (shows only)
Email: xecord@netusa1.net

Antique Quilts/Civil War Items by mail order
Battleground Antiques
Will and Lynn Gorges, Prop.
3910 Highway 70 East
New Bern, NC 28560
(252) 636-3039

Appliqué Patterns
Jeana Kimball's Foxglove Cottage
PO Box 18294
Salt Lake City, Utah 84118

Conservation/Restoration
The Kirk Collection
1513 Military Avenue
Omaha, NE 68111
(800) 398-2542
http://www.kirkcollection.com

Electric Stencil Cutting Knife
Connecting Threads
13118 NE 4th Street
Vancouver, WA 98684
(800) 574-6454

Markers and Machine Quilting Supplies
Keepsake Quilting
Route 25B, PO Box 1618
Centre Harbor, NH 03226-1618
(800) 865-9458
http://www.keepsakequilting.com

Metal Quilting Templates and Marking Pencils
ARDCO templates by QuiltSmith, Ltd
252 Cedar Road
Poquoson, VA 23662-2112
(800) 982-7326

Plastic Feathering Templates
Fons & Porter Quilt Supply
PO Box 171
Winterset, Iowa 50273
(888) 985-1020 (toll free)
http://www.fonsandporter.com

Quilting Books
Quilting Books Unlimited
1911 West Wilson St.
Batavia, IL 60510
(708) 406-0237
http://www.qbu@inil.com
Send $1 for book catalogue.

Quilting Block Books
Crosley-Griffith Publishing Co.
PO Box 512
Grinnel, Iowa 50112
(800) 642-5615
email: crosgriff@aol.com

Quilting and Foundation Piecing Stencils
Graphic Impressions
1741 Masters Lane
Lexington, KY 40515
Send $1 for stencil catalogue.

Quilting and Painting Stencils
Pepper Cory's designs are all from StenSource International and are available at many craft, fabric, and quilt stores. For mail order, contact:
Stencils by Pepper Cory
PO Box 3363
Morehead City, North Carolina 28557
http://www.peppercorystencils.com

Quilting Patterns
Mormon Handicrafts
36 South State Street #220
(in the ZMCI Center Mall)
Salt Lake City, Utah 84111-1482
(800) 843-1480
http://www.mormonhandicraft.com

Quilting Patterns and Batting
Mountain Mist
100 Williams Street
Cincinnati, Ohio 45215-4683
(800)345-7150
http://www.palaver.com/mountainmist/

Quilt Marking Pencils
Roxanne International
3009 Peachwillow Lane
Walnut Creek, CA 94598
(800) 993-4445
http://www.roxanneinternational.com

Quilting Stencils
Needleart Guild
2729 Oakwood
Grand Rapids, MI 49505
(616) 361-1531

StenSource International, Inc.
(800) 642-9293
http://www.stensource.com

Quilt Supplies
The Cotton Patch Mail Order
3405 Hall Lane, Dept. CTB
Lafayette, CA 94549
e-mail: cottonpa@aol.com
(800) 835-4418
(925) 283-7883
A Complete Quilting Supply Store

The Stencil Company
28 Castlewood Dr.
Cheektowaga, NY 14227-2615
(716) 656-9430
Send $1.00 for catalogue
http://www.quiltingstencils.com

Soapstone and Graphite Markers
Morgan Quality Products
30560 Elise Ann
Bulverde, TX 78613

Stencils and Mylar for Making Stencils
Stencils and Stuff
5198 Twp. Rd. 123
Millersburg, Ohio 44654
(330) 893-2499
Send $2 for catalogue.

Water-Soluble Paper
Clotilde,Inc.
B 3000
Louisiana, MO 63353
(800)772-2891
http://www.clotilde.com

Whole-Cloth Designs
Patterns by Jeaneau
PO Box 900127
Sandy, Utah 84090
(801) 942-6764
http://www.quiltit.com

About the Author

Pepper Cory has been a quiltmaker since 1972. She saw an antique quilt at a rummage sale, purchased the quilt for $1.00 and has been making quilts, collecting antique quilts, teaching quilting, and writing quilt books ever since. Her books include *Quilting Designs*

Photo: Mike Galyon

from the Amish, *Quilting Designs from Antique Quilts*, *Crosspatch* (retitled *Multiblock Quilts*), *Happy Trails* (retitled *65 Drunkard's Path Quilt Designs*), and co-author with Susan McKelvey of *The Signature Quilt*. She designs quilting and painting stencils for StenSource International, Inc.

Pepper and her husband, Rod, moved from Michigan to the Crystal Coast of North Carolina in 1996. Along with a lifelong passion for quilting, Pepper enjoys gardening, learning Tai Chi, and walking barefoot on the beach.

Other Fine Books From C&T Publishing

Appliqué 12 Easy Ways! Elly Sienkiewicz
Baltimore Album Quilt Show and Contest, Elly Sienkiewicz
Baltimore Beauties and Beyond (Volume I), Elly Sienkiewicz
Curves in Motion, Quilt Designs & Techniques, Judy B. Dales
Deidre Scherer, Work in Fabric and Thread, Deidre Scherer
Dimensional Appliqué, Baskets, Blooms & Baltimore Borders,
   Elly Sienkiewicz
Free Stuff for Quilters on the Internet, Judy Heim/Gloria Hansen
From Fiber to Fabric, Harriet Hargrave
Hand Quilting with Alex Anderson, Alex Anderson
Heirloom Machine Quilting, Third Edition, Harriet Hargrave
*Make Any Block Any Size, Easy Drawing Methods • Unlimited
   Pattern Possibilities • Sensational Quilt Designs*, Joen Wolfrom
Mastering Machine Appliqué, Harriet Hargrave
Papercuts and Plenty, Vol. III of Baltimore Beauties and Beyond,
   Elly Sienkiewicz
Piecing, Expanding the Basics, Ruth B. McDowell
Quilts for Fabric Lovers, Alex Anderson
Rotary Cutting with Alex Anderson, Tips • Techniques • Projects,
   Alex Anderson
Scrap Quilts, The Art of Making Do, Roberta Horton
Through the Garden Gate, Quilters and Their Gardens,
   Jean and Valori Wells

For more information write for a free catalog from:
C&T Publishing, Inc. P.O. Box 1456, Lafayette, CA 94549
(800) 284-1114 • http://www.ctpub.com •email: ctinfo@ctpub.com

Index